ESSENTIAL
SPEED
READING
TECHNIQUES

ESSENTIAL
SPEED READING
TECHNIQUES

HOW TO BECOME A BETTER, FASTER READER

By Katya Seberson

**ROCKRIDGE
PRESS**

Art Director: Eric Pratt
Cover and interior photography: © domin_domin/iStock
Art Manager: Sue Smith
Editor: Justin Hartung
Production Editor: Ashley Polikoff
Author photo: Courtesy of Katya Seberson

ISBN: Print 978-1-64152-608-1 | eBook 978-1-64152-609-8

To Andrey.
Every girl should get this lucky.

CONTENTS

INTRODUCTION

The idea of speed reading has fascinated me ever since
I was a little girl growing up in rural Russia. As a child,
I was determined to read as fast as my dad, who seemed to
swallow books in a matter of days. He would crack open a
thick Tolstoy novel on Friday evening and be done with it by
the end of the weekend. It looked like magic to me. Sadly, I
did not inherit my dad's "reading genes." On the contrary,
at the age of eight I learned that I was dyslexic. Jarring, I
know. One distinctly embarrassing childhood memory I have
is of scoring 52 words per minute (WPM) on a reading test
while all of my peers scored well over 100 WPM. I was at
least 50 percent slower than the slowest reader in my grade.
And popular methods for teaching dyslexics, such as the
Orton-Gillingham Approach or the Wilson Reading System,
were not yet available where I lived. I just had to muddle my
way through. Later in life, as an adult living in the United
States, not only did I learn how to read English, I learned
how to read fast. Currently, my reading speed varies between
450 and 900 WPM, depending on my familiarity with the
subject matter and my state of mind.

I compare becoming a speed reader to becoming an
athlete—it takes time and practice, but the rewards are
definitely worth the effort. Now, if you are wondering
whether you have to be dyslexic to benefit from this book,
rest assured that you absolutely do not. Indeed, if you are

dyslexic and struggle with decoding words and spelling accurately, I first recommend that you work on that before diving deep into these pages.

Learning to read as an adult gave me a huge advantage in developing my speed reading skills because I could better understand how letters make up words, how words create meaning, and how sentences carry ideas from one to the next. This perspective provided a platform for taking my reading speed to the next level. The best part was, the more I read, the easier and more enjoyable it became. In fact, I liked reading so much that I decided to make a career out of it. I now teach speed reading to adults and teens and have a thriving practice in Midtown Manhattan. I also host a popular YouTube channel where I share my insights on reading and learning with the world.

WHAT TO EXPECT IN THIS BOOK

Speed reading has gotten a bit of a bad rap, so it's important that we set the record straight right out of the gate. In chapter 1, we will debunk myths about speed reading by separating realistic improvements from impossible marketing promises. We'll also identify some factors that make you a slow reader. We will proceed in chapter 2 to determine your current reading speed and comprehension levels, and set a realistic and attainable goal. Having this goal in mind will help you stay motivated and keep track of your progress. Chapter

3 looks at such things as reading environment, books, schedule, eye exercises, and even mind-set—essentials that will set you up for success.

The core of the book is in its exercises, chapters 4 through 8, where you will find proven techniques and practices that will significantly boost your speed and advance your comprehension. As you complete these exercises, you'll start to see an improvement in speed and your ability to grasp information effectively. Ideally, you should practice each exercise for a few weeks before moving on to the next level. Speed reading, just like any other skill, requires practice and time. In chapter 9 you'll get a chance to test yourself and see if you've achieved your goal. And finally, in chapter 10 you will see the different ways that speed reading can be incorporated into your daily life.

Essential Speed Reading Techniques will provide real tools to help you read more quickly, whether you're working your way through an entertaining novel or a challenging textbook. More importantly, the exercises in this book will help you increase your reading comprehension, deepen your understanding of how reading works, and learn why it breaks down and how to get back on track. As you start to read faster and grasp information with ease, you'll begin to enjoy reading more. Let's get started!

WHAT IS
SPEED READING?

Welcome to the world of fast reading! To begin, you're
going to see that speed reading is an achievable skill
and discover some of its history, and you'll gain an
understanding of the anatomy of reading. You'll also take
a look at some of the challenges that slow readers down.
Let's tackle the first chunk: What is speed reading?

Many people mistakenly equate speed reading with masterful skimming, but this definition is wrong. Simply put, speed reading is an advanced form of reading. Just like Olympic marathon running is an advanced form of an existing skill—running—speed reading is an advanced form of reading. An Olympic marathon runner performs the same physical movement as an average runner, but does it faster and more efficiently. Speed reading works the same way.

From this definition, it's clear that speed reading has nothing to do with skimming. Skimming implies skipping words, which is not a technique of true speed reading. Think about it: Would an Olympic runner jump on a bike periodically to get to the finish line faster? No! So why should a speed reader skip words and sentences to get ahead? This misconception has its roots in the history of speed reading.

THE HISTORY OF SPEED READING

The term "speed reading" is closely associated with Evelyn Wood, co-founder of Evelyn Wood Speed Reading Dynamics, a business she established with her husband in the late 1950s. Unfortunately, the way her story unfolded has led many to believe that speed reading is some kind of gimmick.

While teaching at a Utah high school, Wood became concerned about a few underachieving students. And she noticed they had one thing in common—they were all poor readers. Wood built a remedial reading program, helping the students develop a love for words and reading, and then—to her delight—she watched their grades soar. And she made another important observation: The faster the students read, the more they enjoyed it.

Wood's first book, *Reading Skills*, a collaboration with another teacher, came out in 1958, but it didn't produce the speed results she sought. A year later, she touted the use of the hand as a pacer to increase reading speeds, and in 1959, Wood opened her first Reading Dynamics office in Washington, DC. The institute soon started to get big government contracts from the White House. Presidents John F. Kennedy, Richard M. Nixon, and Jimmy Carter all sent staff to Wood's program. As a result, her pacer technique became the much-hyped "secret" to faster reading. Indeed, in 1971 the *New York Times* published an article stating that speed reading had become a permanent feature of education in America.

In a famous TV clip, one of Wood's students was asked to "read" as much of a yet-to-be published novel as she could get through in a minute, and then share what she'd learned. When the time was up, she had made it through 27 pages. And though she'd picked up a few details, including the main character's name and the setting, there wasn't much detailed comprehension. The audience bought it, however, and Wood's method was (falsely) validated. What's important to note here is that Wood's students were skimming rather than reading.

Her company was sold in 1967. The business was growing, yet so was the number of graduates who were feeling frustrated with their expensively acquired skimming skills. By the 1970s, it was clear that this particular version of speed reading was ineffective.

Speed reading's popularity has waxed and waned ever since. In the late 2000s, thought leaders such as Tim Ferris started to espouse speed reading skills using the same old methods, and people were falling for it again. In 2014, new software technologies—including Spritz, a speed reading app, and Readsy, its associated website—made bold claims that readers could increase their speed without sacrificing comprehension. Of course, none of these claims were proven to work, though the public wanted to believe that they did. Later, in 2016 the *New York Times* published an opinion piece called "Sorry, You Can't Speed Read." It was neither surprising nor shocking. Speed reading *isn't* possible when it's taught the way Evelyn Wood suggested. Reading speeds beyond 2,000 WPM are unrealistic without skimming and lifelong training.

The speed reading we are talking about in this book has nothing to do with skimming and requires the reader to read every word. The strategies presented have been scientifically proven and truly help students improve both their reading speed and comprehension. Moreover, they apply to a wide variety of readers, so you can definitely find something that works for you and your specific reading material.

HOW READING WORKS

In order to be a better, faster reader, it's important to understand *how* reading works. While reading, our eyes help us capture reflected light from the page or emitted light from the screen. The captured light then lands on the back of the eye onto a thin, light-sensitive membrane called the retina, where images from the outside world come into a focus. Think of the images as being imprinted on film. For the brain to make sense of the tiny scribbles and shapes, i.e., the text, the light from the page must hit a tiny region of the retina called the fovea, which boasts the highest visual acuity. When light rays land on the fovea, the image can be clearly seen. This is called foveal vision. When they do not, the image may still be seen but with reduced acuity. This type of vision— peripheral vision—is especially weak at distinguishing shapes, which is not ideal for reading.

Once the image is captured on the retina and fovea, the optic nerve sends that information to the brain for further processing and word recognition. Because the fovea is comparatively small, our eyes are unable to take snapshots of whole pages or paragraphs in a way that lets us discern specific details. That's why our eyes unconsciously move from one part of the text to the next as we read.

Let's do a quick experiment. Close one eye and put a finger over the lid. Now, begin reading the text in front of you. You should feel movement below your eyelid. This movement is not continuous; rather, it's unsteady and intermittent. You are experiencing two elements of reading eye movements: **fixations** and **saccades.**

Fixations

Every time your eyes need to capture light from new words to imprint them onto retina, you must keep your gaze in the same location for your brain to process what you're seeing. Think of it as your camera taking the time to focus. Slower readers tend to spend more time on each fixation—they capture less light and therefore often make more fixations per line.

Reading Example
This person is reading the text for understanding. Even though not every word is fixated, the amount of time spent on each word is indicative of the processing of the word.

Skimming Example
This person is skimming the text. This is most obvious from the pattern of fixations that are more dispersed and the shorter fixation durations, which is typical for this type of reading. The main gist of the material may be understood, but poorer memory for the text usually results.

Faster readers need less time to capture light from words, take in more light per fixation, and therefore take in more words per stop and need to pause less frequently on every line.

How much light or, more important, how many words can a person "take in" per individual fixation? Scientists say that the capacity of your individual fixation can vary anywhere between 8 letterspaces to upwards of 22 letterspaces. In practical terms, that's anywhere between one single word to a whole phrase. For example, the phrase "she must go eat dinner" contains 22 letterspaces. If you are taking in 22 or more letterspaces per fixation—which means your eyes only stopped once to capture and recognize the phrase—your eyes would on average stop less frequently than an average American reader.

Saccades

Now let's talk about the next observation you made during your experiment. Your eyes were not only stopping, but also moving. To shift from one fixation point to the next, your eyes need to glide to the right, and this movement is called a saccade. During the saccade, your vision is suppressed, and your brain is busy processing the information you have just taken in during the fixation. Like a camera, the lens closes when you move it to the next picture-taking spot. Saccades vary in length between one-tenth to one-half of a second. The difference in length can be caused by a multitude of anatomical, environmental, and cognitive factors. If you are looking at a large font, for example, your saccades will be different than if you were looking at smaller print.

Regressions

Your eyes also often shift to the left to reread any text that you couldn't fully process. This movement, which happens more than you realize, is called a **regression.** Some eye-tracking devices register a mean of 30 percent regressions out of all eye movements. To illustrate this statistic, imagine that out of 30 minutes of reading, your eyes are rereading the same text for 10 minutes. Reducing regressions will certainly bump up your reading speed, but beware: Reduced regressions may also hinder comprehension.

The average reading speed in America is between 150 and 250 WPM. If you do the math and add up all the time for fixations, saccades, processing, and regressions, the average reader can read 3 words per second. To read 2 to 4 times faster—say, 6 to 12 words per second—speed readers must practice to increase the fixation window, while reducing regressions and the number of fixation stops per line.

Subvocalization

Speed readers are not just constrained by the physical aspects of reading; they must further work on reducing something called **subvocalization**: the inner speech that happens during reading. Some readers whisper or move their lips or tongue during reading. This is called mechanical subvocalization. Other readers just produce silent speech that is known only to them. This is called silent subvocalization.

THE SUBVOCALIZATION DEBATE

There is a debate about whether subvocalization is a mandatory step for comprehension. In our experience, subvocalization is not necessary for comprehension, but can be useful:

1. To help you decode a word with an unfamiliar spelling

2. To help you focus

3. To activate preexisting knowledge on the topic

SPEED READING CHALLENGES

We all learn at different paces and in different ways. Some readers will develop speed reading skills in a matter of weeks, while others will take longer to reach high proficiency levels and might even have to use completely different sets of exercises to achieve similar results. Here are some of the most common roadblocks to faster reading.

Insufficient Vocabulary

Webster's Third New International Dictionary includes roughly 470,000 words. Learning all of them would be impossible, obviously, but increasing your vocabulary will undeniably aid your speed reading efforts. We suggest that you approach the task of improving your vocabulary in a clever way: Look up 100 to 120 high-frequency words that appear in the books and other materials that particularly interest you. Moreover, you should look up words in the dictionary only after you finish a complete section of text such as a paragraph or a sentence.

Note that you're more likely to notice more challenging vocabulary in written language rather than in speech, mostly because writing is a more formal method of communication. Also, your brain tends to disregard unfamiliar words in spoken conversation, filling in the blanks with guesses based on context.

One Size Doesn't Fit All

Much like how athletic shoes are customized to an individual's foot, gait, and activity, your speed reading techniques need to be tailored to your brain, your current level of reading, your familiarity with the subject matter, and the type of text (fiction, nonfiction, etc.) you're tackling. Each type of reading material presents its own rules, patterns, and challenges. For example, many novels follow similar story arcs, whereas an unfamiliar storyline may slow you down as you work to comprehend it. Meanwhile, nonfiction and dense textbooks frequently dive deeply into topics that may be unfamiliar to the reader and require a different pace to absorb the new information. Even your reading platform matters: Online articles and e-books can be a struggle for those with sensitive eyes.

Every individual's brain has an extraordinary and unique set of networks that arrived through genetic endowment and developed as a result of exposure and learning. Even your native language plays a significant role in your reading mind's development. Many researchers say that readers whose native language is non-alphabetic (Chinese or Tamil, for example) use their brains differently when reading.

Before you commit to reading a book, always pause to reflect on your purpose. What are you looking to achieve? Are you reading to find new information or to verify something? Are you reading to learn or entertain yourself? Are you looking to empathize with the author or confront their perspective? Your purpose of reading will predetermine the set of techniques you'll use.

REDEFINING SPEED READING

Remember the Evelyn Wood student we mentioned earlier? She "read" 27 pages of a novel in one minute. Let's do the math, assuming an average of 300 words per page:

300 x 27 = 8,100 WPM

Now that you know the mechanics of reading, you know that reading 8,100 WPM is beyond the ability of the human eye and brain. If the most developed and sharp fovea can only register 22 letterspaces (about 4 words) per fixation, the student must have made 2,025 fixations in that minute to read 8,100 words. That's more than 33 fixations in a second. We also know that fixations take about a quarter of a second, so 33 fixations must take at least eight seconds. We might be overkilling this with math, but you get the point: These speeds are unrealistic and impossible for actual reading with comprehension. The student may have been skimming for a few key details to recall back to the audience.

There's yet another controversial speed reading technique worth mentioning called "photoreading," which claims to give you a quick and easy boost of up to 25,000 WPM by absorbing a whole page in a single glance. But, this math also doesn't even remotely add up. Remember that peripheral vision (the type of vision that photoreading employs) is especially weak at deciphering shapes. Any eye doctor will confirm this. Shapes make letters, letters form words, and words together create meaning in a sentence. If you cannot see the first part—shapes—the chain breaks down. It would be amazing if we could just imprint books onto our memory, but until Elon Musk creates a neurological add-on to our brain, there's no chance.

So is speed reading even possible? Yes. We just need to redefine what speed reading means. As we said before: It's an advanced form of reading where the reader reads every word on the page, just faster and more efficiently. And when we say "reads," we don't secretly mean skim or scan or guess at meaning. We mean clearly see, recognize, understand, and make meaning from text as a whole to help you keep up with your reading for self-improvement, career, and leisure.

SETTING YOUR READING GOAL

Now that you have a deeper, more realistic understanding of speed reading as a skill, it's time to figure out how it applies to your particular brain. You will be learning more about your current reading ability, your eye movements, your comprehension skills, and how you measure up to other readers nationwide. Awareness of your reading strengths and challenges will guide you in your path to becoming a speed reader, so it's highly recommended you take this work seriously. Once you understand where you lose time, you can create targeted drills in order to work on getting faster. Similarly, once you understand where your comprehension dips, you can work on perfecting that sub-skill.

After you know your reading speed and comprehension levels, you'll establish a realistic target for improvement. Make sure you keep this target in the forefront of your mind as you go through the exercises in this book.

FIND YOUR BASELINE

It's test time! You'll find your reading baseline by timing yourself while reading a short story. Keep in mind that we will be testing your reading comprehension afterward, so give it your best effort to understand and remember the details. Please avoid looking ahead and compromising your test results. Remember, this is not a competition or race. It's an opportunity to get to know your brain on reading and see how you can get even more amazing!

You'll notice that the material is not particularly difficult. This is because many other speed reading programs give students a harder passage in the beginning in order to inflate their improvement toward the end.

SPEED TEST

Instructions:

Set aside 15 minutes to do this test and answer the questions. Many of you will not need this much time, but we encourage you to err on the safe side.

- **Find a quiet place where nobody will disturb you for the duration of the test (no pets or kids around).**
- **Read at a table and sit in a chair. Do not do the test while sitting on your couch or lying in bed.**

- Use a stopwatch or phone timer (make sure to turn off all notifications during the test). A pro tip: Make sure you familiarize yourself with how the watch or phone app works before you begin reading.
- Locate the beginning of the text, *The "Genius,"* by Theodore Dreiser, without reading it yet.
- Start the watch and immediately begin reading at your normal pace.
- Pause the stopwatch when you are done.
- Record your time.

Start Reading

From Theodore Dreiser's *The "Genius"*

In one part of this city there lived a family which in its character and composition might well have been considered typically American and middle western. It was not by any means poor—or, at least, did not consider itself so; it was in no sense rich. Thomas Jefferson Witla, the father, was a sewing machine agent with the general agency in that county of one of the best known and best-selling machines made. From each twenty, thirty-five or sixty-dollar machine which he sold, he took a profit of thirty-five percent. The sale of machines was not great, but it was enough to yield him nearly two thousand dollars a year; and on that he had managed to buy a house and lot, to furnish it comfortably, to send his children to school, and to maintain a local store on the public square where the latest styles of machines were displayed. He also took old machines of other makes in exchange, allowing ten to fifteen dollars on the purchase price of a new machine. He also repaired machines—and with that peculiar energy of the American mind, he tried to do a little insurance business in addition. His first idea was that his son, Eugene Tennyson Witla, might take charge of this latter work, once he became old enough and the insurance trade had developed sufficiently. He did not know what his son might turn out to be, but it was always well to have an anchor to windward.

He was a quick, wiry, active man of no great stature, sandy-haired, with blue eyes with noticeable eye-brows, an eagle nose, and a rather radiant and ingratiating smile. Service as a canvassing salesman, endeavoring to persuade recalcitrant wives and indifferent or conservative husbands to realize that they really needed a new machine in their home, had taught him caution, tact, savoir faire. He knew how to approach people pleasantly. His wife thought too much so.

Certainly he was honest, hardworking, and thrifty. They had been waiting a long time for the day when they could say they owned their own home and had a little something laid away for emergencies. That day had come, and life was not half bad. Their house was neat—white with green shutters, surrounded by a yard with well-kept flower beds, a smooth lawn, and some few shapely and broad spreading trees. There was a front porch with rockers, a swing under one tree, a hammock under another, a buggy and several canvassing wagons in a nearby stable. Witla liked dogs, so there were two collies. Mrs. Witla liked live things, so there were a canary bird, a cat, some chickens, and a bird house set aloft on a pole where a few blue-birds made their home. It was a nice little place, and Mr. and Mrs. Witla were rather proud of it.

Miriam Witla was a good wife to her husband. A daughter of a hay and grain dealer in Wooster, a small town near Alexandria in McLean County, she had never been farther out into the world than Springfield and Chicago. She had gone to Springfield as a very young girl, to see Lincoln buried, and once with her husband she had gone to the state fair or exposition which was held annually in those days on the lake front in Chicago. She was well preserved, good looking, poetic under a marked outward reserve. It was she who had insisted upon naming her only son Eugene Tennyson, a tribute at once to a brother Eugene, and to the celebrated romanticist of verse, because she had been so impressed with his "Idylls of the King."

Eugene Tennyson seemed rather strong to Witla père, as the name of a middle-western American boy, but he loved his wife and gave her her way in most things. He rather liked the names of Sylvia and Myrtle with which she had christened the two girls. All three of the children were good looking—Sylvia, a girl of twenty-one, with black hair, dark eyes, full blown like a rose, healthy, active, smiling. Myrtle was of a less vigorous constitution, small, pale, shy, but intensely sweet—like the flower she was named after, her mother said. She was inclined to be studious and reflective, to read verse and dream. The young bloods of the high school were all crazy to talk to Myrtle and to walk with her, but they could find no words. And she herself did not know what to say to them.

Eugene Witla was the apple of his family's eye, younger than either of his two sisters by two years. He had straight smooth black hair, dark almond-shaped eyes, a straight nose, a shapely but not aggressive chin; his teeth were even and white, showing with a curious delicacy when he smiled, as if he were proud of them. He was not very strong to begin with, moody, and to a notable extent artistic. Because of a weak stomach and a semi-anæmic condition, he did not really appear as strong as he was. He had emotion, fire, longings, that were concealed behind a wall of reserve. He was shy, proud, sensitive, and very uncertain of himself.

When at home he lounged about the house, reading Dickens, Thackeray, Scott and Poe. He browsed idly through one book after another, wondering about life. The great cities appealed to him. He thought of travel as a wonderful thing. In school he read Taine and Gibbon between recitation hours, wondering at the luxury and beauty of the great courts of the world. He cared nothing for grammar, nothing for mathematics, nothing for botany or physics, except odd bits here and there. Curious facts would strike him—the composition of clouds, the composition of water, the chemical elements of the earth. He liked to lie in the hammock at home, spring, summer or fall, and look at the blue sky showing through the trees. A soaring buzzard poised in speculative flight held his attention fixedly. The wonder of a snowy cloud, high piled like wool, and drifting as an island, was like a song to him. He had wit, a keen sense of humor, a sense of pathos. Sometimes he thought he would draw; sometimes write. He had a little talent for both, he thought, but did practically nothing with either. He would sketch now and then, but only fragments—a small roof-top, with smoke curling from a chimney and birds flying; a bit of water with a willow bending over it and perhaps a boat anchored; a mill pond with ducks afloat, and a boy or woman on the bank. He really had no great talent for interpretation at this time, only an intense sense of beauty. The beauty of a bird in flight, a rose in bloom, a tree swaying in the wind—these held him. He would walk the streets of his native town at night, admiring the brightness of the store windows, the sense of youth and enthusiasm that went with a crowd; the sense of love and comfort and home that spoke through the glowing windows of houses set back among trees.

He admired girls—was mad about them—but only about those who were truly beautiful. There were two or three in his school who reminded him of poetic phrases he had come across—"beauty like a tightened bow," "thy hyacinth hair, thy classic face," "a dancing shape, an image gay"—but he could not talk to them with ease. They were beautiful but so distant. He invested them with more beauty than they had; the beauty was in his own soul. But he did not know that. One girl whose yellow hair lay upon her neck in great yellow braids like ripe corn, was constantly in his thoughts. He worshiped her from afar but she never knew. She never knew what solemn black eyes burned at her when she was not looking. She left Alexandria, her family moving to another town, and in time he recovered, for there is much of beauty. But the color of her hair and the wonder of her neck stayed with him always.

There was some plan on the part of Witla to send these children to college, but none of them showed any great desire for education. They were perhaps wiser than books, for they were living in the realm of imagination and feeling. Sylvia longed to be a mother, and was married at twenty-one to Henry Burgess, the son of Benjamin C. Burgess, editor of the *Morning Appeal*. There was a baby the first year. Myrtle was dreaming through algebra and trigonometry, wondering whether she would teach or get married, for the moderate prosperity of the family demanded that she do something. Eugene mooned through his studies, learning nothing practical. He wrote a little, but his efforts at sixteen were puerile. He drew, but there was no one to tell him whether there was any merit in the things he did or not. Practical matters were generally without significance to him. But he was overawed by the fact that the world demanded practical service—buying and selling like his father, clerking in stores, running big business. It was a confusing maze, and he wondered, even at this age, what was to become of him. He did not object to the kind of work his father was doing, but it did not interest him. For himself he knew it would be a pointless, dreary way of making a living, and as for insurance, that was equally bad. He could hardly bring himself to read through the long rigamarole of specifications which each insurance paper itemized. There were times—evenings and Saturdays—when he clerked in his father's store, but it was painful work. His mind was not in it.

As early as his twelfth year his father had begun to see that Eugene was not cut out for business, and by the time he was sixteen he was convinced of it. From the trend of his reading and his percentage marks at school, he was equally convinced that the boy was not interested in his studies.

Stop Reading!

Write your time here: _____
*Remember to convert seconds into minutes.
Example: 6 minutes, 10 seconds = 6.166 minutes
To get your WPM, just divide your total word count (1,550) by the minutes (6.166).
For example, your reading speed is 251 WPM if you finished the story in 6 minutes and 10 seconds.

Write your reading speed here: _____

Comprehension Test

This is a two-part test. First, write a summary of the plot, and then answer 10 detail questions. Don't refer back to the text. If you feel like you have to return to the passage, leave the question blank.

Part 1: How Well Did You Understand the Plot?

Please write a three- to five-sentence summary of the story. Include the names of the main characters, their relationship, their actions, and the reasons for their actions. Highlight shifts in time and location changes.

Part 2: Detail Questions

Please choose the answer only if you remember the facts from the text. Skip the question and don't guess if you can't recall the details. Returning back to the text is not permitted.

1. What did Thomas Jefferson Witla do for a living?

   a. worked as a tailor
   b. was an insurance broker
   c. was a salesman for sewing machines
   d. owned a repair shop

2. What type of work did he want his son to take over?

a. sales

b. insurance

c. real estate

d. repairs

3. What animals did Mr. Witla own himself?

a. canary birds

b. cats

c. chickens

d. collies

4. Who was Eugene Witla named after?

a. Chicago senator

b. President Lincoln's father

c. his mom's brother

d. his grandfather

5. One of the girls was named after what?

a. a romantic poem

b. a sweet flower

c. a famous actress

d. her grandmother

6. Who was the youngest of the three kids and the apple of the eye in the family?

  a. Myrtle

  b. Eugene

  c. Sylvia

  d. Miriam

7. What was Eugene's attitude to painting?

  a. he only sketched fragments and never finished

  b. he was very talented and drew still life

  c. he didn't care for painting

  d. he liked to paint images of girls

8. Eugene was in love with one girl's . . .

  a. pretty face and kind manners

  b. black hair and yellow bow

  c. yellow hair and neck

  d. dark eyes and curls

9. Sylvia wanted to be a . . .

  a. writer

  b. painter

  c. teacher

  d. mother

10. **What did Mr. Witla think of Eugene and his business?**
    a. he was convinced Eugene wasn't cut out for it
    b. he was excited about Eugene becoming a businessman
    c. he thought Eugene was better in studies than business
    d. he thought Eugene was better in art and painting than business

Answer Key

Part 1

Your summary should look something like this:

The author is setting the stage and introduces his characters. Thomas Jefferson Witla is a salesman of sewing machines. He is a good businessperson and makes enough money to buy a house and put his kids through school. He has two daughters (Sylvia and Myrtle) and one son (Eugene). His wife, Miriam, thinks highly of him. They have many pets since they both love animals. Eugene is the youngest, and he doesn't have any talent for business. Sylvia gets married and has a kid, while Myrtle is at a crossroads: become a teacher or get married.

If your summary is complete and similar to the example above, give yourself 5 points. If you feel that you are missing a few details, take off a point or two and give yourself 4 or 3 points for the first half of the test. If you feel that your summary is quite different from the examples above, and you feel that you misunderstood the story a little or a lot, give yourself a 2 or a 1. If you wrote nothing, 0.

Write your score for part 1 here: _____

Part 2:

1. C **2.** B **3.** D **4.** C **5.** B **6.** B **7.** A **8.** C **9.** D **10.** A

For each correct multiple-choice question, give yourself half a point. If you answered all 10 questions correctly, you should get a total score of 5. If you made one error or skipped one question, your score is 4.5.

Write your score from part 2 here: _____

Add your scores from both parts together: _____

Example results:

Reading Speed: 251 WPM

Part 1: 5

Part 2: 2 (two errors, four skipped)

Total: $5+2 = 7$

Comprehension: $7 \times 10 = 70\%$

Baseline:

Reading Speed: _____ **WPM**

Comprehension: _____ **X 10 =** _____ %

Read below to figure out how your WPM will affect the rest of your journey through this book.

Below 155 WPM: You are probably losing a lot of time on fixations, regressions, and saccades, and this is great news. This is what this book is focused on. As you go through the rest of the exercises, keep track of your time and try to push yourself to go faster. Specifically, we encourage you to track your regressions and reduce the number of times you reread the text.

Between 155 and 258 WPM: You are probably subvocalizing every single word as you read, because the average speaking speed is about the same 150 to 258 WPM. The exercises in this book will help you tackle subvocalization, and your speed will go up. Additionally, you can bolster your speed by working on widening your perceptual span and reducing regressions.

Between 259 and 310 WPM: You are reading just above the national average and have a great platform to build upon. Chances are you read pretty well already, but you can still improve a few areas to truly enjoy effortless reading. Focus your attention on breaking through subvocalization.

Between 311 and 443 WPM: Great job on breaking through the spoken word barrier. Unlike most readers, you don't subvocalize every word you read. That puts you in a great position for further improvement. Rock on!

Between 444 and 516 WPM: Congrats! Only 5 percent of people in the world can read above 500 WPM, but it doesn't mean you are going to stop here. If you were able to achieve this speed on your own, the exercises in this book will help you get even faster.

Between 517 and 775 WPM: Thank you for joining us in this book! It is very likely that you already enjoy reading and probably do a lot of it for work or pleasure. There are a few advanced exercises in this book that will help you get even faster and more efficient.

776 WPM or above: You may not know this, but you are already in a small group of really fast readers. Especially if your comprehension was 100 percent, you are in a very good position to get even more efficient and take your reading to the next level.

Now let's take a look at your comprehension score.

90 to 100%: Great job. You are certainly well prepared to take your speed to the next level. We will call you a Type 3 reader.

65 to 85%: Well done! You can comprehend well, but may struggle with capturing little details. We will call you a Type 2 reader.

45 to 60%: Nice work! Your comprehension skills are in place, but you need to practice. We will call you a Type 1 reader.

40% or below: Looks like we need to do some work on comprehension. We will call you a Type X reader.

What type of reader are you? Circle your type here:

Type 3   Type 2   Type 1   Type X

PUT A NUMBER ON YOUR GOAL

Now that you have your metrics—reading speed (WPM) and reading type (3, 2, 1, X)—it's time to set a realistic goal for your practice.

If you are Type 3, your reading comprehension skills are intact, and regardless of your current reading speed you can add an extra 300 WPM to it to get your target speed. Example: If you can read at 250 WPM with 90 to 100 percent comprehension (Type 3), your target speed should be 250 WPM + 300 WPM = 550 WPM.

If you are Type 2, your reading comprehension is solid, but it still needs your attention. Aim to add 200 WPM to your current reading speed to get your target speed. Example: If you read at 250 WPM with 65 to 85 percent comprehension (Type 2), your target speed should be 250 WPM + 200 WPM = 450 WPM.

If you are Type 1, your reading comprehension is pretty weak and needs training. Take small steps to increase your speed, and focus more on improving your reading comprehension. For now—until your reading comprehension improves to Type 2 or Type 3—add 100 WPM to your current reading speed to get your target speed. Example: If you read at 250 WPM with 45 to 60 percent comprehension (Type 1), your target speed should be 250 WPM + 100 WPM = 350 WPM.

If you are Type X, reading comprehension should be your main focus, and you should follow all the suggestions in the upcoming chapters without trying to push your speed at all. Once you get more practice, you can repeat the drills in this book with speed as your new focus.

If your results identified you as Type 1 or X, don't despair! As you slow down and master comprehension, you'll be able to achieve even higher gains later and increase your speed.

Please write your target speed here: _____

Finally, keep in mind that your comprehension level will vary from one text to another. In some books, you will be a Type 3, while in others you will be a Type 1 or 2. The exercises in this book will help you develop flexible speeds, similar to the gears in a car, so that you never have to read a scientific research paper and a detective story with the same quickness.

3

GETTING READY TO READ

Now that you have your baseline metrics, it's time to develop a plan for progress. Before we dive deep into the speed reading drills, we will explore some of the essential elements—reading environment, books, schedule, eye exercises and mind-set—that will gear you up for success.

THE IDEAL READING ENVIRONMENT

If you are serious about your speed reading training and want to make it your priority, you must find time in your calendar for training. Some people find that they're able to think more clearly in the morning, but choose what's best for you. Whenever you decide to practice your skills, begin by blocking off 10 minutes in your calendar to practice every day or 25 minutes three times a week. It's important to find time in your calendar and schedule it ahead of time, because if you leave it to chance, you may not ever find a free afternoon when you can practice your speed reading skills.

Plan for the Worst Version of Yourself

To maximize the likelihood of your follow-through on this training, plan for the worst version of yourself to show up, not the best version of yourself. Let's clarify. When we set a goal to do something, it always feels good because the brain is wired for achievement and development. When we make a commitment to improve something, like our reading speed, we feel excited, anticipating the outcomes of our future achievement. Filled with motivation, we make a plan of action where we expect the highly committed version of ourselves—the version of ourselves that never skips a practice session, rationalizes, or makes excuses. However, once we begin working our plan, a different version of ourselves comes to the surface. This "other" person is driven by pleasure and comfort and may want to skip practice sessions or procrastinate. So what can you do? Plan on it happening, because your brain is equally wired to get excited to achieve a new goal to get better and to choose pleasure and avoid exerting extra energy. And you will need lots and lots of mental energy to retrain your brain to process text faster and become a speed reader.

That's why we recommend adjusting your environment to make your practice sessions almost impossible to miss. If you scheduled your practice at the library, agree to meet a friend for coffee nearby or pick up your dry cleaning near the library right after your session. If you practice at home, unplug your Internet router and then turn it on after you have finished your reading practice. You can get a buddy to train with or make a promise with consequences to yourself. Here is a good example of such a promise:

Starting this week, I promise to practice my speed reading drills on Sunday morning, Tuesday morning, and Thursday evening for 25 minutes each session. If I miss a goal by the end of the day, I have to give up Instagram for the next 24 hours.

The idea is to give up something that you enjoy—social media, coffee, movie night, shopping, etc.—as a repercussion for not following through on your plan.

Here is the template for your promise:

Starting _____ ,
I promise _____

_____ .

If I miss a goal by _____ , I have to give
up _____ .

Insert your practice days and a consequence for not doing
what you said you were going to do.

Sit at a Table to Increase Your Focus

Remember that we asked you to sit at a table to perform a
baseline test? To maximize your results, avoid reading in bed
or lying down on a couch. Unbeknown to you, the brain is
scanning the room around you while your foveal vision is
glued to the book. If your peripheral vision catches a glimpse
of your legs or sees the reflection of your body, your brain
will gladly move from so-called "mind awareness" to "body
awareness."

When the brain is in body-awareness mode, the last
thing your brain wants to do is perform the complex
meaning-making activities necessary for reading. Instead,
your brain is scanning your body, focusing on the physical aspects: how tired you are, how tight your muscles
are, how hungry or thirsty, hot or cold, or physically

uncomfortable your body is at this moment. To prevent these messages from entering your brain and messing with your focus while reading, position yourself at a table.

Make sure you sit fairly close to the table and place both feet flat on the floor. This position will prevent you from sitting cross-legged or slouching and interrupting the blood flow to your brain. In fact, many studies show that slouching to the left or right may make subvocalization harder to beat in particular. Depending on your unique brain architecture, your speech centers may be located in the left or right or both hemispheres, and if blood gets unevenly concentrated around these areas, it will be harder to weed out the subvocalization habit. Keeping your spine neutral and your neck even between your shoulders will prevent unnecessary muscle tension in the neck and will keep a steady blood supply for your brain.

If possible, make sure you are facing a blank wall, and sit at a clean and organized desk. If you absolutely have to read in bed, cover your body with a blanket and don't read in a room with a large mirror where you can see yourself. This trick will not work for you if you often fall asleep while reading in bed, as the brain is strongly affected by the environmental clues.

As for lighting, read in a room with ample, soft light to keep from straining your eyes. If you are reading on a device, adjust the font size and screen brightness as needed, avoiding any glare, and, again, make sure you're reading in a room with sufficient light. If you are dealing with eye strain when reading on the computer, try using blue-light-blocking eyewear to relieve tension.

Finally, if noise is a problem for you, avoid practicing in loud spaces or wear noise-canceling headphones.

Reading is an act of empathy with the author, and it requires you to have an open mind. If you have any worries, to-dos, or questions floating around in your head, just write them down to clear your thoughts, and revisit them when you have finished your reading practice.

After the first few practice sessions, reflect back on them and see what you can do to improve. Perhaps you will want to bring a cup of water to your desk or get a tie to control long hair if it's a distraction.

USING FOCUS CARDS

One of the hardest things about reading is focusing on one task for an extended period of time. Focus cards can be very helpful if you struggle with a "monkey mind" syndrome when you read. Focus cards are a fancy name we gave to blank flash cards or scratch paper that you keep nearby during your reading practice. If a thought comes to mind that screams for attention, simply write it down on a focus card instead of acting on it.

We get good at what we practice, and if you practice getting distracted, you will get good at distracting yourself. For many people, distractibility and loss of focus are learned habits. When something seemingly important comes to mind, quickly write it down on a focus card and continue with your reading practice. This will ensure that you don't forget your thought, free up some mental space, and eventually interrupt the habit. When you are done with your reading exercise, go ahead and look through your focus cards and batch those small tasks: order more batteries, pay the phone bill, and check your appointments. If reading is not your favorite pastime, your brain will especially seek relief from it and send you all kinds of peculiar suggestions. Expect it to happen and write them down on a focus card. After a hundred of these records, you will notice a significant reduction of internal requests for attention, and your focus will improve.

EYE WARM-UPS

You've already learned about the jumpy eye movement called a saccade. However, your eyes are also able to move continuously when following a moving object. Close one eye again and place a finger over it. Stretch your other hand in front of you and keep your thumb up. Keep your gaze on the nail of your thumb and move your arm smoothly to the right and back to the middle. Your eyes should be able to follow your hand without making any jumps. This movement is called "smooth pursuit." To read faster, you will use both saccades and smooth pursuit, so it's important to know how they both feel.

Before starting the exercises, warm up your eyes with these two exercises:

Crazy Eight

Pick a point on the wall about 10 feet in front of you, and focus on it. Trace an imaginary figure eight with your eyes with that point in the middle. Keep tracing for four times, then switch directions.

Near and Far Focus

Stretch your arm and hold your thumb in front of your face, and focus on it for five seconds. Find an object far away from you, and focus on that for five seconds. Return your focus to your thumb. Repeat five times.

CHOOSE THE RIGHT BOOKS

To complete the exercises in this book, some texts will be provided, but you'll also need to choose a few books to practice with on your own. Many people make the mistake of selecting the most complex and boring books in their library. On the contrary, you should pick books that will be fun to read. If you like cheesy novels, go for it!

Books you choose for training should be in a familiar subject area. If you work in finance and know nothing about coding, stay away from textbooks about programming. Being familiar with the topic gives your brain the advantage of recognizing words and phrases and quickly mapping them to meaning. Also, the complexity of the language and syntax should be below your current reading level. Unless you are an English professor with Type 3 comprehension and a baseline speed of over 400 WPM, you shouldn't be choosing books that have sentences more than three lines long.

As we are about to dive deep into the training, remember that your brain will be applying effort to create meaning from text and do it at a faster rate. Brains are much better at making meaning from short sentences—the type of sentences that seem similar to spoken speech. Just like a runner wouldn't start training for a marathon with an obstacle course of 30 miles, you shouldn't start your speed reading training with a complex book that will kill your momentum and drive. We encourage you to choose your practice books carefully and stay away from difficult material, but we also suggest that you don't overthink it. Give yourself an hour to pick one or two books to practice on, and get going.

Now that you have a plan of action, ideal environment, and materials for training, let's get to the exercises that will take your reading to the next level.

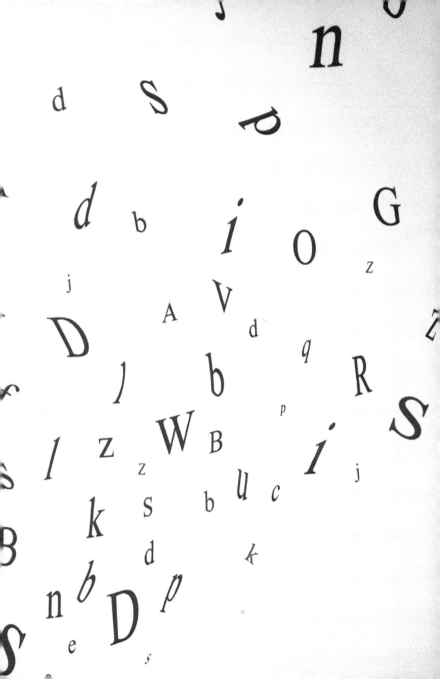

THE WORD-CLUSTERING TECHNIQUE

When studying the eye movements of faster readers, researchers noticed that their subjects fixated on groups of words at a time instead of individual words, making fewer stops per line of type. This phenomenon is called word clustering, and it's the most effective technique for becoming a speed reader. Anybody can learn how to cluster words together when they read. However, we need to be careful to prevent losing comprehension, which is a result of clustering words at random.

When scientists discovered that faster readers cluster words together, they intuitively assumed that if slower readers could learn to fixate on two or three words at a time, they would also be able to read and understand text faster. Unfortunately, it doesn't work that way. Less frequent stops per line is not the cause of faster reading speed. Rather, speed readers possess superior language processing skills. Therefore, mastering word clustering must begin with honing your visual language processing skills.

To start, let's learn some simple word clusters—sets of words that create meaning as a group. This technique is universal and will help you improve regardless of your current reading speed and type. Simple examples of word clusters include phrases like "in the morning," "at the convention center," and "of the test scores."

All these phrases begin with a preposition (words like of, in, at, with, from, etc.) and end with a noun (a person, animal, or thing). In grammar, these word clusters have a name that speaks for itself—prepositional phrases; we will call them prepositional clusters. Feel free to look up a full list of prepositions online to help yourself locate prepositional clusters in text. Fun fact: "Of" is the most frequently used preposition in the English language. Once you spot "of" in your text, know that this is the beginning *of your prepositional cluster.* Pun intended!

Let's now do a quick practice exercise:
Identify six clusters in the next paragraph. Draw brackets around them. It's essential that you not only spot prepositions but also outline the clear boundaries of the word cluster. Remember, they always begin with a preposition and end with a noun.

At the beach, people relax with various activities: lying in the sun, jumping over the waves, and enjoying the company of their friends.

Answer Key

[At the beach], people relax [with various activities]: lying [in the sun], jumping [over the waves], and enjoying the company [of their friends].

If you created larger clusters like [lying in the sun] or [jumping over the waves], that's great news because it means you're starting to see larger sets of words that create meaning together.

Now, try again. This time, we hid seven prepositional clusters:

In this introductory harmonica class, you'll be learning from the most experienced teacher at this music school. He began his professional training at the tender age of six, when he insisted on taking harmonica lessons with his older brother. Now he boasts more than 20 years of teaching experience.

Answer Key

[In this introductory harmonica class], you'll be learning [from the most experienced teacher] [at this music school]. He began his professional training [at the tender age of six], when he insisted on taking harmonica lessons [with his older brother]. Now he boasts more than 20 years [of teaching experience].

Prepositional clusters are easy to spot and will give you a better sense of what's important in the sentence and what's secondary. For example, the main "actor" and "action" of the sentence—the subject and the verb—will never appear inside of a prepositional cluster. Words that carry the most essential meaning (subject/verb) will always be outside of the prepositional cluster.

Now open your practice book and read for 10 minutes, taking note of the prepositional clusters in the text. You can even use a pencil to bracket them off. As you begin to identify prepositional clusters, you'll start to minimize your fixations and maximize your speed. Once you get familiar with the way prepositional clusters look in text and the content they provide, your brain will automatically start perceiving them in one fixation.

ADVANCED WORD CLUSTERING TECHNIQUE

Let's take your knowledge of words and meaning to a deeper level. The most frequently used word in the English language is the definite article "the." Interestingly enough, "the" is the word that opens the majority of written sentences. *The* reason for this seems obvious: Most sentences begin with the subject—usually a noun—that needs an article in the English language. Therefore, if you spot a definite article with a capital T, you must be certain that the subject or the main "actor" of the sentence will follow. *The recognition of this sign will help you cluster words together intelligently instead of doing it by accident.*

Try clustering some words in this paragraph:
The hidden path became narrower. Because of the fragrant flowers, we both began to sneeze uncontrollably, and we walked in the opposite direction toward Columbus Circle. The annoying allergies made us come back to the hotel room. The trip to the nearby pharmacy helped, but we didn't feel like going back to the blooming Central Park for the next three days. From that one visit, we always associate Central Park with pollen-filled tears.

Answer Key

[The hidden path] became narrower. [Because of the fragrant flowers], we both began [to sneeze uncontrollably], and we walked [in the opposite direction] [toward Columbus Circle.] [The annoying allergies] made us come back [to the hotel room.] [The trip to the nearby pharmacy] helped, but we didn't feel like going back [to the blooming Central Park] [for the next three days.] [From that one visit,] we always associate Central Park [with pollen-filled tears.]

Notice that when a sentence does not begin with an article "the" or "a," it usually begins with an opening cluster like "Because of the fragrant flowers." Usually, this phrase will be offset by a comma and followed by the main actor of the sentence. You can use this trick to help yourself with comprehension and locate the main actor of the sentence if it doesn't show up at the very beginning.

In the example below, opening and prepositional clusters have been emphasized in the first three paragraphs to help you get used to recognizing them faster. In paragraph four, try to continue reading and follow the pattern.

When I reached high school, I reluctantly joined DECA, an academic team preparing emerging business leaders **in marketing, finance, hospitality, and management**, as I had a mild interest **in the business world** and also saw it **as an opportunity to get away** from everything **going on at home**. However, I instantly found my niche **in finance** as it allowed me **to utilize my skills** successfully **with numerical data** and fed my interest **in the stock market**.

After experiencing DECA to its fullest—competing **at state conference**, the online stock market challenge, and being a part **of the leadership team**—I wanted **to share the knowledge** I had gained, specifically **in finance**. My friend and I started a Financial Literacy Club **at our school**, which stressed the importance **of money management** and its numerous effects. We created personalized budgeting spreadsheets **for college and beyond**, allowing individuals **to be financially secure**.

For the longest time I did not want to accept **that my life was different**. However, participating **in these activities** helped me realize the uniqueness **of my hardship**. I was able to find the fine line **of becoming independent** and supporting my family. My outlook **on the entire situation** shifted as I began **to embrace it** rather than resent it.

Reflecting upon these hard times, my family received so much support from family friends. They would pick me and my sister up from school and drop us off at home while my dad was at work, feed us so my dad wouldn't have to cook after a long day at work, and countless other things. These small acts of kindness have had a lasting impact on me, which I am forever grateful for.

Turn to your book again and practice clustering words together while paying attention to the beginnings of sentences, the article "the," and the opening clusters. Whenever a sentence begins with "the," make sure to fixate on a few words that follow to make advanced clusters.

If you find this technique difficult, don't give up! We will revisit this topic in the later chapters. For now, look at the written text of the following sentences and try to analyze how meaning gets created from sets of words. Remember, the content doesn't usually come from individual words, but rather from collaborations between words and their interaction with each other. If grammar isn't your strong suit and English classes evoke painful memories, we encourage you to develop your own unique clustering method that is based on meaning and comprehension.

HOW DO I KNOW IF I AM GETTING FASTER?

In your own book, you will want to calculate the average number of words per line. Take three full lines and count every single word. Let's say you counted 45 words in those three lines. Now, divide that number by three, and you'll get the average count of words per line—in this case, 15 words per line.

This number will help you calculate your WPMs and track your progress. Set the timer for one minute and read at your normal pace. Mark where you stopped and count the number of full lines you've read. Let's say it's 10. Multiply the average word count per line (15) by the number of lines you read in a minute (10) to get your initial WPM (150 WPM).

After you practice with clustering for a few days, measure your speed again at the end of the session. Your improvements will vary based on your current reading speed and reading level, but you should be seeing an improvement anywhere from 50 to 250 WPM from the word-clustering practice.

5

REDUCING SUBVOCALIZATION

Do you say words silently in your head when you read? Most people say they do. It's like asking, "Can you feel your heartbeat?" You start tuning into your pulse and feeling it for a while in response to the prompt. Because people are poor judges of their cognitive processes, many readers—even the fastest ones—mistakenly believe that they always sound out words in their head as they read. Many speed reading programs take advantage of this: They begin to condemn subvocalization as a bad habit and train readers to unlearn it as a rudimentary skill no longer needed for reading. The latest research, however, shows that subvocalization is essential to reading comprehension. Still, there are forms of subvocalization that will slow you down, and these should be reduced.

Mechanical subvocalization is one such impediment. If you find yourself moving your lips when you read or humming along with the author, you are a mechanical subvocalizer. This type of subvocalization contributes to both slower speeds and comprehension loss. Mechanical subvocalization happens when you start to act out your brain's suggestions to sound out the words on the page, and the nerve impulses go all the way from your brain to your vocal cords or your lips. If you don't want to subvocalize mechanically, make sure that your mouth and throat don't perform any specific movement in response to the text you are reading. The extreme way to unlearn this habit is by holding a pencil between your teeth. While uncomfortable, this method is extremely effective at interrupting the pattern of reading with your lips moving. If you find yourself moving your lips, read this chapter with a pencil between your teeth.

If you are not noticing any movement in your mouth, that's great news, but it doesn't mean that your subvocalization can't be reduced even further. Think back to the last time you watched a movie with subtitles. Were you subvocalizing with the actors, or did you switch to silent reading at some point? Most foreign movie fans have no problem following the plot on the screen and visually reading without any inner speech involved. How do we know this? The next time you're in a movie theater watching a film with subtitles, look around the room 15 minutes after the movie has begun. By that time, most moviegoers will have flipped the switch to silent, reading visually with no lip movement unless they are enjoying the last bits of popcorn.

This is an example of the brain's ability to connect the spelling of words to their meaning, bypassing the inner voice. The switch often flips subconsciously when you find yourself deeply absorbed in a book. Your eyes begin to speed up and look at the squiggles on the pages and your brain automatically responds by creating meaning from them, similar to making a movie inside of your head.

It's important to note that even the fastest, most skilled readers begin reading every time with a bit of subvocalizing. But once they get comfortable with the text, they increase their speed to the point where subvocalization becomes annoying, and their inner speech subsides and sometimes even stops. This phenomenon is called crossing the spoken word barrier. The reader has surpassed the speed of reading out loud and begins to read visually.

Many readers who have developed great decoding skills should be able to read visually without a lot of subvocalization. If you are a Type 2 or 3 reader, reading anywhere from 150 to 350 WPM, this is your main assignment in this book. You can break the spoken word barrier! If you are a Type 2 or 3 who reads a lot faster than 350 WPM, this will also be fun for you. For Types 1 and X with 149 WPM and slower speeds, we encourage you to keep working on your clustering skills and hold off on the subvocalization practice for now. Once your speed increases to 150 WPM and you feel more comfortable comprehending what you read, feel free to give it a shot. We've deliberately introduced subvocalization after you've learned about clustering. When you master clustering, i.e., perceive many words at one fixation, it will become harder to subvocalize since you can't say several words at the same time.

Remember the two eye movements we discussed earlier, saccade and smooth pursuit. You've learned that saccade is the choppy movement our eyes use to read text. In the next exercise, we will introduce some elements of smooth pursuit to increase speed and help you break the spoken word barrier. To activate smooth pursuit, simply glide your eyes at an average rate from the left margin to the right margin. Do that for a few seconds without reading, and just glide your eyes over text. Remember this physical feeling of smooth pursuit in your eyes; it will help you push your eyes to go faster. If you can, try to notice prepositional and opening clusters as you move along the text. In the upcoming exercise, we will emphasize some clusters to help them stand out on the page and make your job a little easier.

In the next exercise, we will be reading an article by Leo Babauta called "A Guide to Habit Resilience." Your assignment is to read the text just a tiny bit faster by trying to push your eyes along the lines using smooth pursuit. The text has 1,000 words. Estimate how long it will take you to read this much text if you increased your speed by

15 percent. If your baseline was 250 WPM, divide 1,000 by 250 X 1.15 [1,000/(250*1.15)], which equals three and a half minutes. When you read, try to make that time and remember the feeling of smooth pursuit to help yourself move forward at this new speed. Start the timer, and start reading.

Start Reading

I've coached thousands **of people** who want **to change habits,** and I've found there's a key difference between those who actually make changes **and those who don't.**

That key difference is what I like to call "habit resilience."

Habit resilience is the ability **to bounce back** when things don't go as you planned, **to stay positive,** to encourage yourself, **to forgive yourself,** to be loving and compassionate with yourself, **to shake it off** and start again afresh. To learn and grow from struggles.

The opposite **of habit resilience** is getting discouraged **when things don't go** as planned, beating yourself up, trying not to think about it **when you mess up**, ignoring problems, complaining, blaming others, deciding you can't change, hardening your low or harsh opinion **of yourself.**

Let's look **at one example:**

I want **to change my eating habits,** which is pretty tough to do . . . so I set myself a plan to eat oats **for breakfast,** a salad **for lunch,** and scrambled tofu with veggies **for dinner.** Great! But then **during the week,** I have to go to a work get-together, a family party, a 3-day trip **to New York,** and then my daughter's birthday party. All the plans went out the window **on those days.**

So at this point, I can give up, beat myself up, ignore the problem . . . or if I've developed habit resilience, I can shake myself off, make some adjustments **to the plan,** give myself some love, encourage myself, and start again, keeping a positive attitude the whole time. The second way **of doing it** will result in long-term change—if you can stick with it, there's no change you can't create.

That's just one version **of habit resilience,** but you can see the difference **between the first option and the second one** is huge.

So how do we develop habit resilience? Let's take a look.

The good news is **that you can develop** this marvelous quality or skill of **habit resilience.** Actually, it's a set of skills, but they can be developed with some practice.

Here's how to develop habit resilience:

- Loosen your hold **on expectations.** When we start **to make changes** in our lives, we often have unrealistic expectations. Six-pack abs **in four weeks!** But when we actually try **to hit those expectations,** we usually fall short. **At least**, at first. **Over the long run,** we can often make greater changes than we think we can. **But over the short term,** the changes are small, and not very orderly either. Change is messy. So just expect things **to go less than ideally.** Don't be too attached **to how you expect** things to go, so that when your expectations aren't met, you can just take it in stride.

- Learn the skill of adjusting. If your diet plan doesn't go as planned, it's not necessarily a fault **of yours**— it's the fault of the method or plan. How can you make it better **to accommodate your life?** Maybe you can get some accountability, set up some reminders, get rid **of junk food** from you house, and so on. There are a thousand ways **to adjust a plan** or method. **When things go wrong,** look for a way **to adjust,** don't just give up.

- Practice self-compassion and forgiveness. This is so important, but most people have the opposite habit— **when things go wrong,** we often beat ourselves up, are critical and harsh. **Those kinds of reactions** are unhelpful and can keep us stuck **in old habits for years.** Instead, we need to learn **to be kinder to ourselves** when we don't measure up **to what we hope** we'll be. When we let ourselves down, it's important **to forgive ourselves.** Be compassionate, seeing our own suffering and **wishing for relief** from that suffering. Wishing for peace for ourselves. Being loving to ourselves, no matter what we do.

- Don't ignore problems, face them **with kindness.** That said, being forgiving is very different than just pretending it didn't happen. If we've gone off our exercise plan, or stopped meditating . . . don't just ignore the problem, not wanting to face it. Instead, turn towards the problem, and look **at it with kindness.** It's like if you have a crying child — is it better **to ignore the child** and just hope that they'll shut up? That will just lead to more pain **for both of you.** Instead, give them a hug. Acknowledge their pain. Give them love. Be there **for them.** And do the same for yourself when you're having difficulties.

- Learn **to encourage yourself.** We need **to practice this** regularly. **When you falter,** can you be encouraging **to yourself?** Can you stay positive **in the face of failure?** Can you look at it as another step **in your growth,** instead **of failure?**

- Find encouragement from others. **In the same way,** we can get encouragement **from other people.** Ask for help **from friends and family.** Find a good friend who will help you get back **on track, with love.** We are not alone—lots **of others know** what it's like to struggle, and are willing **to support us** when we're struggling.

- Learn perseverance—keep coming back. Stay positive when things go astray, and just keep coming back **to the habit** you want to change. Want **to quit smoking** but you backtracked when your father died? Get back on it **as soon as you're able.** Come back **with even more resolve.** Commit yourself even deeper.

Can you feel that **if you practice these skills,** you'll handle any difficulty **that comes your way?** That your path to change might be bumpy, filled **with obstacles,** but nothing will stop you **if you keep a positive attitude,** keep coming back, keep being loving and compassionate with yourself?

This is habit resilience. And it will change your entire life, if you practice.

Stop Reading!

Now let's do a quick comprehension test. Please write a couple of sentences summarizing the article. What is habit resilience, and how do you develop it?

Answer Key

Your paragraph should look something like this:

Habit resilience is the ability to bounce back when things don't go as planned; it's the main differentiating factor between people who change habits and those who don't. To develop habit resilience, learn to face problems instead of pretending they don't exist, learn to adjust, feel self-compassion, and learn to encourage yourself and recommit in the face of adversity.

If you were able to maintain a slightly higher speed and your summary matches the answer key, we encourage you to take your practice to your own reading material. Make sure you have at least 20 minutes of uninterrupted time to enjoy your book and train yourself to reduce subvocalization and reinforce clustering. Try to read 15 to 25 percent faster with full comprehension. If you normally read four pages in five minutes, go for five pages in five minutes for your practice. We encourage you to give subvocalization 15 to 30 practice sessions of 20 minutes or more. In those sessions, you want to teach your brain to break the barrier of spoken word and maintain comprehension without inner speech.

If you didn't make the time or misunderstood the text when you read faster, turn the dial back and slowly increase your speed. In your book, if you usually read four pages in five minutes, try to read four and a half pages in five minutes for your practice. There is no rush in retraining your brain; let it adjust to the new speed. Boost your pace once you start to feel more comfortable at a faster rate and keep adding.

WHAT TO EXPECT

If you picked the right book for your reading level, you could experience reduced subvocalization on the first day of practice. After a few minutes of reading at a slightly higher rate, your brain will adapt and let go of subvocalizing every word. The switch is seamless, and you will probably not experience any sensation along with it, especially if you are deeply engaged in the plot. When you start to read consistently at a higher rate, trying to achieve complete understanding, your brain will make some biological changes in its wiring to save time and optimize processing. Instead of sounding out the words in your head and then listening to your inner voice, your brain will start seamlessly mapping written words to the phonetic code and accessing meaning. When that happens, you will notice that your focus and comprehension improve as you take less and less time to finish your reading material.

Subvocalization, however, will never go away completely. Even when you start reading faster than 500 WPM, your brain will want to subvocalize certain words from time to time. Sometimes, you will need some help in decoding a word with an unfamiliar spelling that your visual brain doesn't recognize, and subvocalization can help you access the word. Sometimes, your mind will start to drift, and the inner voice will help you refocus. Other times, the brain will get very excited to activate preexisting knowledge on the topic or a concept and shout the names of ideas it already knows a lot about.

STOPPING REGRESSION

Many people try to reread text once they feel that they've lost comprehension. One of the common reasons for comprehension loss is failing to track pronouns. Pronouns are words that point to nouns without naming them. Here is a good example of a pronoun in a sentence: "This feels right." "This" is a pronoun that is pointing to something mentioned earlier in the text but doesn't name it exactly. If you fail to identify what "this" is referencing, you may end up getting lost in the book and having to read again. Fast and effective readers try to quickly map back their pronouns to keep up with the author's thought.

Here are some examples of sentences with pronouns:

We invited **everyone we** could think of to surprise **her**. Naturally, **we** missed **someone** important, and **she** was upset about **that** at first. **We** called **him** right away, and when **he** finally showed up, **everyone** laughed about **it** together.

Tip to fix: Every time you see a pronoun in a sentence, take a quick note of it and make sure you know exactly what this pronoun refers back to.

6

THE REDUCED MARGIN TECHNIQUE

In our discussion of How Reading Works (page 7), we examined the anatomical limitation of our eyes and how little text they can perceive per individual fixation—the number of letterspaces your fovea can perceive varies anywhere from 4 to 22 depending on the font, lighting, and your visual acuity. The **reduced margin** technique is an adjustment to the way you move your eyes along the line to help you maximize the amount of text your eyes can take in during individual fixations. As you can probably guess, it has something to do with margins.

Most printed materials have margins—the space between the main text on a page and the page's edge. When online articles first emerged, web programmers underestimated the importance of margins for the reader and populated the web with margin-less pages. A few years later, it became crystal clear that margins significantly impact the readability of digital text, and they were added to most online blogs and website templates. Although margin-less web pages still exist, it is generally understood today that having wide enough white space around text is critical for readability.

If margins are so imperative, why are we talking about reducing them? Even though having margins is crucial for easier reading, we must realize that they don't contain any text and therefore don't require sharp foveal vision. Peripheral vision will do since all we need from margins is to decipher where lines begin and end. To take advantage of your peripheral vision on margins, begin to consciously move in or indent your initial and final fixations on each line. To make it easier, imagine two vertical lines running down the page over the text about half an inch from the outside inward. These lines are your approximate anchors for your first and last fixations on each line.

By indenting your initial fixation along with last fixations on each line of reading, you will activate your peripheral vision and engage your eyes more. You will also be engaging your brain's ability to make meaning from a text when you are indenting your fixations. It is especially useful to have mastery of common language clusters—prepositional and opening clusters—to help you capture more words per individual fixation. Many readers find this exercise eye-opening and start to see immediate gains in speed and focus. If you are reading a text of low difficulty, it should be pretty easy to indent your fixations and minimize your fixations without losing any comprehension.

Here is how the eye movement of an average reader changes when using the reduced margin technique. Below is the image of eye fixations with and without the reduced margin technique. If each blue circle signifies a fixation, can you guess which one is which?

The weather was improving after the drought, and the forecasts were looking promising for crops.

The weather was improving after the drought, and the forecasts were looking promising for crops.

Notice that the first example was read with only four fixations, while the second example was read with six fixations. Naturally, the first was read faster. By now you probably realize that the first used the reduced margin technique and the second one didn't.

Now, it's your turn to try. Read the following text and remember to align your fixations with the lines.

Flight is a phenomenon that has long been part of the natural world. Birds fly not only by flapping their wings, but also by gliding with their wings outstretched for long distances. Smoke, which is composed of tiny particles, can rise thousands of feet into the air. Both of these types of flight are possible because of the principles of physical science. Likewise, man-made aircraft rely on these principles to overcome the force of gravity and achieve flight. Lighter-than-air craft, such as the hot air balloon, work on the buoyancy principle. They float on air much like rafts float on water. The density of a raft is less than that of water, so it floats. Although the density of water is constant, the density of air decreases with altitude. The density of hot air inside a balloon is less than that of the air at sea level, so the balloon rises. It will continue to rise until the air outside of the balloon is of the same density as the air inside. Smoke particles rise on a plume of hot air being generated by a fire. When the air cools, the particles fall back to Earth.

In order to fly an object must have "lift," a force moving it upward. Lift is usually made by wings according to the Bernoulli Principle. The Bernoulli Principle describes how the speed of air and the pressure in the air are related. When the speed goes up, the pressure goes down and the opposite is also true.

How did it go? If it felt uncomfortable, you are doing it right. The reduced margin technique requires activating a new area in your eyes, the parafovea. The parafovea is a thin belt that surrounds your fovea, the part of your retina that you normally use for reading. It is not nearly as sensitive to details as the fovea and, as such, is unable to distinguish words. However, the parafovea has a great ability to detect shapes and is definitely superior to the rest of the eye's periphery.

The retina has yet another outer belt called the perifovea, which also contributes to peripheral vision. Parafoveal vision is peripheral vision that uses the parafovea area of the retina—located between the fovea (sharp-detailed vision) and the perifovea (less-detailed peripheral vision)—and is involved in the mechanism of planning fixations. Because of its ability to detect shapes, the parafovea can "read" the shapes of words and clusters and make predictions about a better landing for the next eye fixation. By optimizing your fixations, you will reduce your stops per line and maximize your reading comprehension. Developing your parafoveal vision takes time and training, just like any other habit. Therefore, we encourage you to practice in your own material for a few weeks to achieve significant improvement. Initially, you can even draw the vertical lines with your pencil to keep reminding your brain to reduce the margins.

ADVANCED PARAFOVEAL READING

You can use the periphery of your retina to not only reduce the number of fixations per line, but also to preview the material ahead. As you are reading the text, your eyes are seeing the words and spaces on the current line, and your retina and brain are capturing two to three lines outside of foveal vision. You can tap into this information to help yourself preview the text ahead and even plan your fixation stops. As we mentioned earlier, parafoveal and perifoveal vision are not nearly as sharp as foveal, but they can still register shapes and boundaries of words pretty well. Some words, like "knowledge" and "occasionally," have a very specific shape and length, while prepositions, like "in," "at," and "of," are short little bits surrounded by white spaces and signify the beginning of a cluster. With practice, your brain will get better at registering them with your peripheral vision and adjust your eye movements accordingly.

Here is a quick demonstration of the reach of parafoveal vision compared to foveal:

Anna Pavlovna's drawing room was gradually filling. The highest Petersburg society was assembled there: people differing widely in age and character but alike in the social circle to which they belonged. Prince Vasili's daughter, the beautiful Helene, came to take her father to the ambassador's entertainment; she wore a ball dress and her badge as maid of honor.

Small circles represent fixations (foveal vision).

Large circles represent available information (parafoveal vision).

To tap into this ability, first you need to become aware of it. Second, you need to master clustering (which we covered in chapter 4 beginning on page 49) and basic English sentence structure to make better inferences from looking at word shapes, punctuation marks, capital letters, and spaces. We will be covering basic sentence structure later in chapter 8 (page 91). For now, incorporate the near and far focus eye exercises discussed in chapter 3 (see page 44) into your daily practice, and start paying attention to the lines below your current reading focus. Especially notice capital letters and periods, as they signify the beginning of a new sentence and therefore a new thought.

After a few weeks of practicing with your material, you'll experience a speed boost of 5 percent or more as a response to your brain's increasing ability to preview upcoming text and therefore optimize fixations on the line. Even though 5 percent faster may not seem like a lot, remember that small improvements add up to massive differences.

LAYERED (MULTIPLE) READING

In this chapter, you will learn how to improve your overall performance on harder texts using a layered reading approach. This process involves three steps: inspect, read, and reflect.

Reading is an act of empathy. Whether you're reading fiction or nonfiction, the author is taking you on a journey, and your job as a reader is to follow along. Some journeys are like a walk in the park (think of an easy read that you enjoy), while others are more like a tough run on an obstacle course (think complex academic material). Whereas walks in the park don't require a particular plan, tough races demand a trusted map that you study ahead of time along with an accurate GPS you'll use in the moment. When authors don't provide clear maps and GPS systems for their writing, they often leave behind many clues to help you construct one of your own and prime your brain for reading. So, to better understand the writer's argument hidden in an academic book, you would first approach the book as an inspector.

INSPECT

First, take a look at the title and subtitle. Imagine what the book is about before you even crack it open. What do you think the author is trying to communicate about the topic on the cover? Next, consider the publication date. This is especially important when reading time-sensitive materials like scientific research or technical publications. You may even change your mind about reading the book if it was published too long ago to still be relevant.

You'll also want to note who published the book. With the proliferation of self-published titles, it's important to keep in mind that books that have a publisher usually undergo more rigorous editing and fact checking. It's always important to read with a critical eye, but this is especially important when reading a self-published book. On the other hand, books by big-name publishers will likely be quite different in nature, and knowing the publisher will help you mentally place the book in a category. The more you read, the more you'll get a sense for it.

Of course, it's the author that really gives a book its unique identity, so it's essential to learn about their background. What makes the author an expert on a subject? Why should you listen to the author's message? Do some Internet research. While an interview with the author may have little or nothing to do with the text you're reading, it can be a great way to get the gist of the author's argument.

Authors do so much promotion for their books that it's relatively easy to find interviews on podcasts and YouTube. And because authors often use the best examples from their books in these interviews, they can be a perfect primer for the brain. Starting to read with some pre-gained knowledge about the writer's perspective will help you comprehend the book's content more quickly.

Is There a Table of Contents? Treat It Like a Map

Remember how we said that the author would give you a map of the argument? Where is the book taking you? How are you getting "there"? How many large parts and mini components does the argument have? It's all in the table of contents. It's amazing how many people just dive into reading without even glancing at the contents page, whereas the author has spent considerable time coming up with a detailed outline, and nonfiction books often can't be sold without having a comprehensive table of contents. If you are reading a white paper without a table of contents, flip or scroll through it. Even though the outline is usually constant (Abstract, Introduction, Existing techniques, Author's contribution, Results, and Conclusion), it's a good idea to see which parts make up the lion's share of writing and therefore will be the main focus of the argument.

Is There an Index? Skim It

The index helps you understand the language of the book. Reading the index will not only give you an idea for the range of topics covered, but it will also tell you the other people the book connects to and the jargon used. Perhaps you'll spot some background knowledge required to comprehend the argument.

Identify Pivotal Points

At this point, you have an overview of the journey the author is taking you on (from the table of contents) and of the jargon (from the index). It should be relatively easy to identify the pivotal points of the argument and identify corresponding chapters. Alternatively, you can try reading the first chapter and looking for a summary and the locations of central points. It's customary for nonfiction writers to outline their books in the introductory pages. This book is no exception, as we provided such a summary on page ix in the section called What to Expect in This Book.

Exercise

Take 10 minutes today to perform a quick inspection process for your practice book and write down your takeaways.

READ

Once you've finished your inspection, you can start your reading journey, keeping the central ideas in mind. As you read, carry the summary of the argument with you. If the author promised to demonstrate how a concept plays out in different environments, that's what the reader should expect to see. Effective readers always keep the author accountable for delivering on the book's initial promise. If you get lost after reading a chapter, not knowing what to make of it, feel free to access your GPS, i.e., the table of contents, to see how that author fits this mini component into the argument.

If you find yourself disagreeing with the author loudly in your head, we encourage you to continue reading. Remember that reading is an act of empathy, and while you are reading, it's helpful to think of the author as a good friend who is telling you a story. You wouldn't interrupt a friend just because you disagree with what they said. As you read, always make sure you mark places in the book where you contest the argument or get confused, while separating them from the places you value and would like to commit to memory. We recommend reading physical books with multicolored sticky notes on hand—they serve as a bookmark as well as a memory tool: dark colors for confusing paragraphs and bright colors for memorable ones. Reading tablets offer very similar systems of bookmarks that can be color-coded, so feel free to devise your own system.

REFLECT

When you finish reading the book, you are not done with it yet. It's time to revisit your tabs and reread some portions of the text. Now that you have fully heard the author's argument from beginning to end, you may be able to better understand some confusing parts in light of the new knowledge or perspective. Sometimes, you will be triggered to reread a large chunk of the book, and that's okay.

Lastly, with the utmost bravery, write a brief paragraph to summarize the main points of the book. Some people like to keep their collection of thoughts in a catalog system like Goodreads or Evernote. There you can make references to particular pages and chapters and outline your takeaways.

Reflection upon the novelty of the book as well as your personal opinion is essential to your development as a reader and thinker, so please don't skip this step.

Exercise

Visit Amazon, Goodreads, or another website with book reviews and search for the title of your practice book. Look at the results and skim through other readers' summaries. Commit to making a summary of your own once you finish reading the book.

TIPS FOR READING ON-SCREEN

On-screen reading can put a bigger strain on your eyes than reading a physical book for many reasons, including blue light exposure, distracting ads, and font variability.

To combat blue light, consider wearing blue-light-canceling glasses if you read on your laptop. Additionally, relieve eye strain by taking five-minute breaks every 25 minutes, looking away and maintaining a far focus. This is known as the Pomodoro technique.

Palming is another great exercise that can help you reset your eyes when you read on-screen. Here's how it's done:

1. Warm up your hands and cup your palms

2. Close your eyes and place your cupped palms over them

3. Make sure no light is coming through between your fingers and nose

4. Open your eyes and stare at the darkness

5. Keep your eyes bathing in the darkness for 30 seconds

Visit my YouTube channel, *Seberson Method*, to see a demonstration of the palming technique.

Make sure you are using a good ad blocker on your browser. There are many free browser extensions that can convert an online article filled with advertisements to a clean text-only document.

Many reading devices have settings for font size and background color. Use a beige or neutral-colored background to reduce the contrast between white and black.

UNDERSTANDING HOW TEXT CREATES MEANING

There is one more puzzle we need to solve before you can be well on your way to becoming a speed reader: How text creates meaning. The major difference between people who succeed in learning to speed read and those who do not is rooted in this understanding. Students with extensive prior experience in reading seem to subconsciously know how written text converts into comprehension, while nonreaders are often left to grapple, which makes them doubt their abilities, slow down, and reread. Since reading comprehension is the foundation for why we read, it's not surprising that frequent readers who have good comprehension are more likely to graduate from this training as speed readers than nonreaders. This chapter will be essential for both frequent readers and nonreaders, as we will cover some hacks readers of any level can use to unpack the meaning of long and confusing sentences and navigate complex writing.

SPOKEN LANGUAGE VS. WRITTEN LANGUAGE

As we touched upon earlier, it's the exposure to printed material, the frequency of reading, that primes the brain for future advancement in speed reading. Notice that we are exclusively talking about exposure to written words and not spoken speech—that makes a huge difference! It's also important to note that this isn't about intelligence or IQ: Some very intelligent and well-spoken people who are nonreaders fail to develop speed reading skills quickly because they lack the significant experience with reading and print that frequent readers have. Many people find this confusing, and here is why: Mistakenly, they think of written text as if the author spoke into a microphone, and then their free-flowing speech was transcribed and recorded in writing right away. Wrong! Written text and spoken speech are very different. Sadly, due to the anatomical limitation of the human brain, even the smartest people on the planet do not express themselves in errorless, text-like, complex sentences with adverbial phrases and deliver their ideas in complete coherent paragraphs.

The reason impromptu verbal expression appears less complex than writing is because the human brain is quite weak at producing spoken speech, and extemporaneous speech is often filled with utterances, errors, and repeats. Because of this limitation of the brain, we rarely hear complex issues presented in unprepared speech using advanced sentence structures, complex sentences, and complete paragraphs. However, almost any text is filled with these grammatical structures. That's why nonreaders, who usually rely on spoken communication for learning (TV news, podcasts, YouTube videos, online classes, or lectures), have a harder time adjusting to the rules of written text. Printed material does not equal spoken language written down; written text has rules and major differences that frequent readers pick up automatically, while nonreaders need to be made aware. Don't worry if you think of yourself as a nonreader; we will be covering those differences in this chapter.

ADVANTAGES OF WRITTEN TEXT

Printed text does not only make comprehension harder; written text also offers a lot of advantages to the reader and the reader's brain. Spoken speech is fleeting and requires the listener to follow the speaker. Conversely, written text can provide a sense of control as the reader can choose the speed of processing—slowing down on some specific words and phrases or speeding up through others. You can even reread the same page if you like, whereas you can rarely ask the speaker to repeat themselves at any point in their speech. Another advantage of written text is the freedom to pause and look up unfamiliar words. We usually don't have the privilege of being able to interrupt the speaker to ask for a definition of an unknown term. Written text also combats auditory bias where your brain "unhears" unfamiliar words just to stay on track with the speaker's main message. Punctuation is another phenomenon that's unique to written text, and learning to leverage punctuation—colons, dashes, commas, ellipses, brackets, etc.—is another tactic in reading comprehension.

POTENTIAL STUMBLING BLOCKS FOR NONREADERS

Among the many hindrances for nonreaders, such as weird spellings and inconsistent punctuation, overly long sentences seem to be the primary star on the hit parade. Take this example from Tolstoy's *War and Peace*:

The thought immediately occurred to him that his promise to Prince Andrew was of no account, because before he gave it he had already promised Prince Anatole to come to his gathering; "besides," thought he, "all such 'words of honor' are conventional things with no definite meaning, especially if one considers that by tomorrow one may be dead, or something so extraordinary may happen to one that honor and dishonor will be all the same!"

Or consider this contemporary example by Vartan Gregorian:

Whether inscribed on rock, carved in cuneiform, painted in hieroglyphics, or written with the aid of the alphabet, the instinct to write down everything from mundane commercial transactions to routine daily occurrences to the most transcen-dent ideas—and then to have others read them, as well as to read what others have written—is not simply a way of transferring information from one person to another, one generation to the next. It is a process of learning and hence, of education.

The reason these long continuous lines of text appear confusing to some nonreaders and almost call for multiple rereads is simple: People don't often communicate in spoken speech using these grammatical structures. On top of it, many readers don't know how to unpack the meaning of the sentence and break it apart. To understand the unpacking mechanism, we must first discuss how meaning is created in a sentence—you must first be a good reader to become a speed reader.

HOW MEANING GETS CREATED

Before we begin digging into English grammar, we want to preface this discussion of linguistics by saying that we have intentionally simplified the content to make it accessible to a wider audience. The syntax of the English language is quite simple. To create a meaningful sentence, we only need two components: the "actor"—or the subject—and the "action"—the verb. The closer these two components are in the sentence, the easier they are to spot.

Identify the subject and the verb in this sentence: Prince Anatole promised Prince Andrew to come to his gathering.

Prince Anatole is the "actor," i.e., the subject of the sentence. The "actor" is performing the "action" of promising, and "promised" is the verb in this sentence. It's important that the subject and the verb are connected grammatically for the sentence to make sense.

Prince Anatole promised Prince Andrew to come to his gathering.

Now, what is Prince Andrew? "Prince Andrew" is the object receiving the action, while "to come to his gathering" is a combination of additional phrases. After reading chapter 4, you should be able to identify those as clusters.

Prince Anatole promised Prince Andrew to come to his gathering.

Let's try to find the subject and the verb in this sentence:
The promise to attend Prince Andrew's gathering is of no account to Pierre.

The subject is "the promise," and the verb here is "is."

The promise to attend Prince Andrew's gathering is of no account to Pierre.

Do you see how the subject and the verb are further removed from each other? Even though it's still pretty easy to make sense of this sentence, you are starting to see the stumbling blocks. Another interesting thing about this sentence is that it doesn't have an object; it has a complement, "of no account." The promise is of no account.

The promise to attend Prince Andrew's gathering is of no account to Pierre.

Everything else in this sentence is additional clusters.

SHRINKING LONG SENTENCES

The easiest way to combat the stumbling blocks with long sentences is to shrink the drawn-out lines and constrain them to the four main parts of the basic sentence structure.

SUBJECT   **VERB**   **COMPLEMENT/ OBJECT**   **ADDITIONAL PHRASE**

Exercise

Read this long sentence and shrink it down to the basics: subject, verb, complement/object, and additional phrase.

The women of Montgomery, both young and older, would come in with their fancy holiday dresses that needed adjustments or their Sunday suits and blouses that needed just a touch—a flower or some velvet trimmings or something to make the ladies look festive.

Write your basic sentence here:

_____

_____

Answer Key

1. Women would come in with clothes for adjustments.

2. Women brought clothes for adjustments.

Let's go through the shrinking process together. The subject was easy to spot, as the definite article "the" started the sentence. "The women" are the actors on the sentence. The verb "would come in" is separated from the subject by the additional phrase "both young and older."

The women of Montgomery, **both young and older**, would come in **with their fancy holiday dresses** that needed adjustments **or their Sunday suits and blouses** that needed just a touch—a flower or some velvet trimmings or something to make the ladies look festive.

There are two interesting components in this sentence. The first component is the word "that." When writers use the word "that," they usually add an essential detail about the preceding word, and this sentence was no exception: "holiday dresses that needed adjustments" and "suits and blouses that needed just a touch." The author is almost pointing to essential information about dresses, suits, and blouses with the word "that." Knowing this trick can help you unpack the meaning of lengthy sentences.

Tip: When you see a drawn-out sentence, scan it first and try to spot the word "that" and be sure to connect whatever phrases follow it to the preceding words.

The women of Montgomery, both young and older, would come in with their *fancy holiday dresses* that needed adjustments or their Sunday *suits and blouses* that needed just a touch—a flower or some velvet trimmings or something to make the ladies look festive.

The second component of the practice sentence we'd like to highlight is the dash (—). Remember, punctuation exclusively exists in written text and provides multiple hints for the reader to better interpret the message. Even though dashes have many uses, one of the primary purposes of dashes is to provide clarifications, similar to "let me tell you more about that." Indeed, in the example sentence, it may be helpful to think of the dash as an arrow. As in "let me tell you more about that touch."

Let me tell you more about that touch

needed just a touch—a flower or some velvet trimming or something to make the ladies look festive.

Interpreting the dash as an arrow will help you unpack the main meaning of the sentence and see clearly what's most important and what's secondary. Otherwise, the reader may get lost between the flowers and the velvet trimmings and consider those to be the main content of the sentence. Now that you know this about dashes, every time you see one in a long sentence, you can interpret it as "let me tell you more about that" and attribute the information after the dash to the word immediately in front of it.

Exercise

Let's now tie it all together in a practice excerpt from Leo Babauta's "The Age of Distraction." Read the text on the next page carefully and identify some components we discussed in this chapter. Keep an eye out for:

- **Dashes**
    - that offset additional phrases on both sides
    - that say "let me tell you more about that"
- **Subjects**
    - that are removed from their verbs
    - that appear after a long opener
    - that appear at the very beginning of the sentence
- **Semicolons**
    - that add a new independent idea
    - that separate items on a list
- **Word Clusters**
    - opening clusters
    - prepositional clusters
- **Conjunction "that"**
    - adding new essential detail to the word immediately before.

Start Reading

While humanity has never been free of distraction—from swatting those bothersome gnats around the fireplace to dealing with piles of paper mail and ringing telephones— never have the distractions been so voluminous, so overwhelming, so intense, so persistent as they are now. Ringing phones are one thing, but email notifications, Twitter and Facebook messages, an array of browser tabs open, and mobile devices that are always on and always beeping are quite another. More and more, we are connected, we are up to our necks in the stream of information, we are in the crossfire of the battle for our attention, and we are engaged in a harrying blur of multitasking activity. When we're working, we have distractions coming from every direction. In front of us is the computer, with email notifications and other notifications of all kinds. Then there's the addicting lure of the browser, which contains not only an endless amount of reading material that can be a black hole into which we never escape, but unlimited opportunities for shopping, for chatting with other people, for gossip and news and lurid photos and so much more. All the while, several new emails have come in, waiting for a quick response. Several programs are open at once, each of them with tasks to complete. Several people would like to chat, dividing our attention even further.

Answer Key

- **Dashes**
    - that offset additional phrases on both sides
        - While humanity has never been free of distraction—from swatting those bothersome gnats around the fireplace to dealing with piles of paper mail and ringing telephones—the distractions have never been so voluminous, so overwhelming, so intense, so persistent as they are now.
    - that say "let me tell you more about that"
        - When we're working, we have distractions coming from every direction—in front of us is the computer; to the side is the smartphone; on our wrist is the smartwatch.
- **Subjects**
    - that are removed from their verbs
        - Ringing phones that became the extension of our arm are one thing
    - that appear after a long opener
        - While humanity has never been free of distraction—from swatting those bothersome gnats around the fireplace to dealing with piles of paper mail and ringing telephones—the distractions have never been so voluminous, so overwhelming, so intense, so persistent as they are now.
    - that appear at the very beginning of the sentence
        - Several programs are open at once

- **Semicolons**
    - that add a new independent idea
        - the more we are connected, the more we are up to our necks in the stream of information; we are in the crossfire of the battle for our attention, and we are engaged in a harrying blur of multitasking activity.
    - that separate items on a list
        - from every direction—in front of us is the computer; to the side is the smartphone; on our wrist is the smartwatch.
- **Word Clusters**
    - opening clusters
        - All the while,
    - prepositional clusters
        - of reading material
- **Conjunction "that"**
    - adding new essential detail to the word immediately before.
        - an endless amount of reading material that can be a black hole from which we never escape.

In your own material, turn to a brand-new paragraph, and preview the paragraph by scanning it as a whole before reading it. How many sentences does it have? How long are they? Does the paragraph have colons or dashes? Try to spot some of the conjunctions and curious punctuation, and relate it to meaning. This will help you prime your brain for reading this paragraph and paint an initial picture of the content. Previewing paragraphs is an invaluable technique for reading academic material with complex sentence structures. Identifying key components such as subject, verb, complement or object, and additional clusters will help you unpack meaning faster and allow you to navigate difficult material with ease.

CHECKING YOUR GOAL

As we are getting closer to the finish line, let's revisit chapter 2, page 35, and remind ourselves of our initial target speed and comprehension. What type of reader were you when you started reading this book? Let's find out what type of reader you are now. For accuracy, we chose an excerpt from the same reading material as the first baseline test: *The "Genius,"* by Theodore Dreiser.

Earlier, you read the text for good comprehension and answered a few questions at the end. The same assignment is awaiting you here, but the story is about three times shorter. The total word count is 612. Start the timer and start reading.

COMPREHENSION
READING TEST A

Start Reading

Eugene's experience with girls had not been very wide. There were those very minor things that occur in early youth—girls whom we furtively kiss, or who furtively kiss us—the latter had been the case with Eugene. He had no particular interest in any one girl. At fourteen he had been picked by a little girl at a party as an affinity, for the evening at least, and in a game of "post-office" had enjoyed the wonder of a girl's arms around him in a dark room and a girl's lips against his; but since then there had been no re-encounter of any kind. He had dreamed of love, with this one experience as a basis, but always in a shy, distant way. He was afraid of girls, and they, to tell the truth, were afraid of him. They could not make him out.

But in the fall of his seventeenth year Eugene came into contact with one girl who made a profound impression on him. Stella Appleton was a notably beautiful creature. She was very fair, Eugene's own age, with very blue eyes and a slender sylph-like body. She was gay and debonair in an enticing way, without really realizing how dangerous she was to the average, susceptible male heart. She liked to flirt with the boys because it amused her, and not because she cared for anyone in particular. There was no petty mean-ness about it, however, for she thought they were all rather nice, the less clever appealing to her almost more than the sophisticated. She may have liked Eugene originally because of his shyness.

He saw her first at the beginning of his last school year when she came to the city and entered the second high school class. Her father had come from Moline, Illinois, to take a position as manager of a new pulley manufactory which was just starting. She had quickly become friends with his sister Myrtle, being perhaps attracted by her quiet ways, as Myrtle was by Stella's gaiety.

One afternoon, as Myrtle and Stella were on Main Street, walking home from the post office, they met Eugene, who was on his way to visit a boy friend. He was really bashful; and when he saw them approaching he wanted to escape, but there was no way. They saw him, and Stella approached confidently enough. Myrtle was anxious to intercept him, because she had her pretty companion with her.

"You haven't been home, have you?" she asked, stopping. This was her chance to introduce Stella; Eugene couldn't escape. "Miss Appleton, this is my brother Eugene."

Stella gave him a sunny encouraging smile, and her hand, which he took gingerly. He was plainly nervous.

"I'm not very clean," he said apologetically. "I've been helping father fix a buggy."

"Oh, we don't mind," said Myrtle. "Where are you going?"

"Over to Harry Morris's," he explained.

"What for?"

"We're going for hickory nuts."

"Oh, I wish I had some," said Stella.

"I'll bring you some," he volunteered gallantly.

She smiled again. "I wish you would."

She almost proposed that they should be taken along, but inexperience hindered her.

Eugene was struck with all her charm at once. She seemed like one of those unattainable creatures who had swum into his ken a little earlier and disappeared. There was something of the girl with the corn-colored hair about her, only she had been more human, less like a dream. This girl was fine, delicate, pink, like porcelain. She was fragile and yet virile. He caught his breath, but he was more or less afraid of her. He did not know what she might be thinking of him.

Stop Reading!

Write your time here: _____ *

*Remember to convert seconds into minutes. Example:
1 minute, 10 seconds = 1.166 minutes
To get your WPM, just divide the total word count (612) by the minutes (1.166).

For example, your reading speed is 528 WPM if you finished the story in 1 minute and 10 seconds.

Write your reading speed here: _____

Comprehension Test

This is a two-part test. First, write a summary of the plot, and then answer five detail questions. Don't refer back to the text. If you feel like you have to return to the passage, leave the question blank.

Part 1: How Well Did You Understand the Plot?

Please write a three- to five-sentence summary of the story. Include the names of the main characters, their relationship, their actions and reasons for their actions. Highlight shifts in time and location changes.

Part 2: Detail Questions

Please choose the answer only if you remember the facts from the text. Skip the question and don't guess if you can't recall the details. Returning back to the text is not permitted.

1. How old was Eugene when he met Stella?

    a. sixteen
    b. twenty-one
    c. seventeen
    d. fourteen

2. What originally attracted Stella to Eugene?

    a. his looks

    b. his shyness

    c. his sister

    d. his career

3. Where was Eugene heading when he stumbled on Stella and Myrtle?

    a. to Harry Morris's house

    b. home

    c. to his father's store

    d. to school

4. What did Eugene volunteer to bring?

    a. hickory tree

    b. hickory nuts

    c. hickory candy

    d. grilled corn

5. Who was Stella's father?

    a. the school principal

    b. a manager at a pulley manufacturer

    c. a post office worker

    d. the mayor of Illinois

Answer Key

Part 1:

Your summary should look something like this:

Eugene encounters his sister's friend Stella on the street as he is walking over to his friend Harry's. Stella is being very nice to him, and they have a brief exchange about the hickory nuts, and he starts to feel infatuated. Stella seems to like him back.

If your summary is complete and similar to the examples above, give yourself 5 points. If you feel that you are missing a few details, take off a point or two and give yourself 4 or 3 points for the first half of the test. If you feel that your summary is quite different from the examples above, and you feel that you misunderstood the story a little or a lot, give yourself a 2 or a 1. If you wrote nothing, 0.

Write your score for part 1 here: _____

Part 2:

1. C 2. B 3. A 4. B 5. B

For each correct multiple-choice question, give yourself a point. If you answered all five questions correctly, you should get a total score of 5. If you made one error or skipped one question, your score is 4.

Write your score from part 2 here: _____

Add your scores from both parts together: _____

> **Reading Speed:** 451 WPM
> **Part 1:** 5
> **Part 2:** 3 (one error, one skipped)
> **Total:** 5+3 = 8
> **Comprehension:** 8 X 10 = 80%

Baseline:
> **Reading Speed:** _____ WPM
> **Comprehension:** _____ X10 = _____ %

If you have reached your goal, congratulations! If you haven't reached your goal yet, revisit some of the chapters and keep practicing. In your own material, always strive to push your eyes to go faster as long as you maintain good comprehension. The best measure for good comprehension is when you can explain what you've read out loud, in complete sentences, with your notes closed. If you can give a coherent and accurate summary, you are maintaining solid comprehension.

READING COMPREHENSION TEST B

Set the timer and start reading.

Start Reading

The second meeting happened on Saturday evening as arranged, when he came home from his odd day at his father's insurance office. Stella had come to supper. Eugene saw her through the open sitting room door, as he bounded upstairs to change his clothes, for he had a fire of youth which no sickness of stomach or weakness of lungs could overcome at this age. A thrill of anticipation ran over his body. He took especial pains with his toilet, adjusting a red tie to a nicety, and parting his hair carefully in the middle. He came down after a while, conscious that he had to say something smart, worthy of himself, or she would not see how attractive he was; and yet he was fearful as to the result. When he entered the sitting room, she was sitting with his sister before an open fire-place, the glow of a lamp with a red-flowered shade warmly illuminating the room. It was a commonplace room, with its blue cloth-covered center table, its chairs of stereotyped factory design, and its bookcase of novels and histories, but it was homey, and the sense of hominess was strong.

Mrs. Witla was in and out occasionally, looking for things which appertained to her functions as house-mother.

The father was not home yet; he would get there by supper-time, having been to some outlying town of the county trying to sell a machine. Eugene was indifferent to his presence or absence. Mr. Witla had a fund of humor which extended to joking with his son and daughters, when he was feeling good, to noting their budding interest in the opposite sex; to predicting some commonplace climax to their one grand passion when it should come. He was fond of telling Myrtle that she would one day marry a horse-doctor. As for Eugene, he predicted a certain Elsa Brown, who, his wife said, had greasy curls. This did not irritate either Myrtle or Eugene. It even brought a wry smile to Eugene's face for he was fond of a jest; but he saw his father pretty clearly even at this age. He saw the smallness of his business, the ridiculousness of any such profession having any claim on him. He never wanted to say anything, but there was in him a burning opposition to the commonplace, a molten pit in a crater of reserve, which smoked ominously now and then for anyone who could have read. Neither his father nor his mother understood him. To them he was a peculiar boy, dreamy, sickly, unwitting, as yet, of what he really wanted.

"Oh, here you are!" said Myrtle, when he came in.

"Come and sit down." Stella gave him an enticing smile. He walked to the mantel-piece and stood there, posing. He wanted to impress this girl, and he did not quite know how. He was almost lost for anything to say.

"You can't guess what we've been doing!" his sister chirped helpfully.

"Well—what?" he replied blankly.

"You ought to guess. Can't you be nice and guess?"

"One guess, anyhow," put in Stella.

"Toasting pop-corn," he ventured with a half-smile.

"You're warm." It was Myrtle speaking. Stella looked at him with round blue eyes.

"One more guess," she suggested.

"Chestnuts!" he guessed.

She nodded her head gaily. "What hair!" he thought. Then—"Where are they?"

"Here's one," laughed his new acquaintance, holding out a tiny hand.

Under her laughing encouragement he was finding his voice. "Stingy!" he said.

"Now isn't that mean," she exclaimed. "I gave him the only one I had. Don't you give him any of yours, Myrtle."

"I take it back," he pleaded. "I didn't know."

"I won't!" exclaimed Myrtle. "Here, Stella," and she held out the few nuts she had left, "take these, and don't you give him any!" She put them in Stella's eager hands.

He saw her meaning. It was an invitation to a contest. She wanted him to try to make her give him some. He fell in with her plan.

"Here!" He stretched out his palm. "That's not right!" She shook her head.

"One, anyhow," he insisted.

Her head moved negatively from side to side slowly.

"One," he pleaded, drawing near.

Again the golden negative. But her hand was at the side nearest him, where he could seize it. She started to pass its contents behind her to the other hand but he jumped and caught it.

"Myrtle! Quick!" she called.

Myrtle came. It was a three-handed struggle. In the midst of the contest Stella twisted and rose to her feet. Her hair brushed his face. He held her tiny hand firmly. For a moment he looked into her eyes. What was it? He could not say. Only he half let go and gave her the victory.

"There," she smiled. "Now I'll give you one."

He took it, laughing. What he wanted was to take her in his arms.

Stop Reading!

Write your time here: _____ *

*Remember to convert seconds into minutes. Example:
2 minutes, 15 seconds = 2.25 minutes
To get your WPM, just divide the total word count (820) by the minutes (2.25).

For example, your reading speed is 356 WPM if you finished the story in 2 minutes and 25 seconds.

Write your reading speed here: _____

Comprehension Test

This is a two-part test. First, write a summary of the plot, and then answer five detail questions. Don't refer back to the text. If you feel like you have to return to the passage, leave the question blank.

Part 1: How Well Did You Understand the Plot?

Please write a three- to five-sentence summary of the story. Include the names of the main characters, their relationship, their actions and reasons for their actions. Highlight shifts in time and location changes.

Part 2: Detail Questions

Please choose the answer only if you remember the facts from the text. Skip the question and don't guess if you can't recall the details. Returning back to the text is not permitted.

1. How important to Eugene was his father's presence?

a. Eugene was concerned about his father's absence
b. Eugene was indifferent to his father's presence or absence
c. Eugene preferred to have his father's absence
d. Eugene preferred to have his father's presence

2. When joking, Mr. Witla would predict that Myrtle will one day marry a . . .

    a. banker

    b. lawyer

    c. insurance agent

    d. horse doctor

3. What did Eugene think about his parents' ability to understand him?

    a. Eugene felt understood

    b. Mrs. Witla understood him, while Mr. Witla didn't

    c. Eugene felt misunderstood by both parents

    d. Eugene felt belittled by his parents

4. What was Stella doing in the commonplace room with Myrtle?

    a. toasting hickory trees

    b. toasting chestnuts

    c. toasting popcorn

    d. arm wrestling

5. What did Eugene feel like doing at the end of the contest?

    a. enjoying his prize

    b. hugging his sister

    c. hugging Stella

    d. going back to his room

Answer Key

Part 1:

Your summary should look something like this:

The author first talks about Eugene and his family, revealing that Eugene doesn't think highly of his father and feels quite misunderstood. Then, he has a flirty fight over chestnuts with his sister Myrtle and Stella, her friend. He feels very infatuated with Stella.

If your summary is complete and similar to the example above, give yourself 5 points. If you feel that you are missing a few details, take off a point or two and give yourself 4 or 3 points for the first half of the test. If you feel that your summary is quite different from the examples above, and you feel that you misunderstood the story a little or a lot, give yourself a 2 or a 1. If you wrote nothing, 0.

Write your score for part 1 here: _____

Part 2:

1. B **2.** D **3.** C **4.** B **5.** C

For each correct multiple-choice question, give yourself a point. If you answered all five questions correctly, you should get a total score of 5. If you made one error or skipped one question, your score is 4.

Write your score from part 2 here: _____

Add your scores from both parts together: _____

> **Reading Speed:** 356 WPM
> **Part 1:** 5
> **Part 2:** 4 (one skipped)
> **Total:** 5+4 = 9
> **Comprehension:** 9 X 10 = 90%

Baseline:

> **Reading Speed:** _____ WPM
> **Comprehension:** _____ X10 = _____ %

SPEED READING
FOR LIFE

Reading isn't something to be done once a week to check a box—it's something to do every day in order to improve and invest in yourself. Reading is by far the most common factor that successful people across the globe share. Charlie Munger, Warren Buffett's longtime business partner at Berkshire Hathaway, once said, "In my whole life, I have known no wise people (over a broad subject matter area) who didn't read all the time—none, zero." If reading books gives wisdom, speed reading is akin to gaining accelerated wisdom, but you have to do it.

To help you develop a consistent practice of speed reading, we encourage you to establish a daily reading routine: 25 pages every day. You can read more, but no less. To make that happen, you must make sacrifices and find time to read. Reflect back on your last 24 hours, and think of how you have spent them. At any point in the last day, could you have been more productive and made time for a quick but invaluable reading practice? If you struggle to find time, track how much of it you spend watching TV, shopping, or browsing social media, and cut that time in half. Use the remaining time for daily reading.

What will the 25-pages-a-day habit get you? First, you will read a book like Ashlee Vance's biography of Elon Musk in two weeks or less. Second, you will never be confused about how long a book will take you to finish, no matter how lengthy it is. For example, just by looking at *Seveneves* by Neal Stephenson, you'll be confident in saying that you can get through his 880 pages of brilliant prose in about a month. This helps you pacify your brain into knowing that this book can be read, especially if long books used to have a terrifying effect on you. Third, having a 25-pages-a-day habit gives your brain a certain goal to move toward every time you read. Knowing that you have committed to getting through that many pages daily will help you move past some fatigue and distractions. The brain likes the feeling of completion and achievement. Lastly, if you stick with this habit, you will add 10 to 12 more books a year to your reading diet and your intellect.

To engage with the reading world, become an active member of websites like Goodreads, or join a book club and actively participate in reading challenges. Being surrounded by other frequent readers will give you a sense of comfort and help your brain relax into reading more. A lot more. In some ways, becoming a speed reader is similar to changing your identity—changing your thinking, making different choices, spending time reading, and focusing on improving yourself.

To ensure that your reading comprehension is on point, find reviews and compare your comprehension with others'. If you struggle to comprehend a book or an article, read what other people say about it, and then reread the whole thing. This experience will reveal what you've missed and help you improve your reading technique in the future. You are your best teacher.

Finding time for reading doesn't have to be hard, but you have to make sure you have a book with you at all times. It might be on your phone, Kindle, or even a physical book. Waiting for a bus? Stop staring down the street and read. Waiting in line? Read. On the train? Read. Waiting for your flight or sitting on the plane? Read.

If you are someone who likes reading different books at the same time, we have a solution for you as well. We recommend reading five to 10 pages in each book at a time. We like to suggest that you read something timeless in the morning, such as Dale Carnegie's *How to Win Friends and Influence People*, Stephen Covey's *The 7 Habits of Highly Effective People*, Marcus Aurelius's *Meditations*, or maybe a spiritual text or scripture. This type of timeless wisdom will set your mind in the morning and center you like a mini meditation would.

At lunchtime, we recommend reading a nonfiction book complementary to your career or field of interest. If you are a programmer, reading a textbook about AI would be absolutely beneficial. In the evening, we recommend winding down with a biography or an autobiography of someone you admire or want to be more like. The magic of these books consists in their marriage of storytelling and lessons. A good example of such a book is *Principles*, by Ray Dalio, which beautifully combines fascinating life stories and revealing anecdotes along with important ideas to ponder. This is a perfect adult version of a bedtime story.

Advertising tycoon David Ogilvy once said that education can be "a priceless opportunity to furnish your mind and enrich the quality of your life." Now that you are reading faster and more effectively, you can fulfill both of these needs with more enjoyment and a sense of accomplishment. Additionally, you can have a variety of reading speeds at your disposal. So, if you wish to speed up through a portion in a textbook, you can do so without any loss of comprehension. Similarly, you can choose to slow down on some portions of text and subvocalize intentionally, especially if you want to connect deeply with the words and the wisdom they provide.

SPEED READING APPS

You can find plenty of speed reading apps on the market, but there is a scarcity of apps that actually work. Most apps are based on the RSVP technology, which has been around for almost a decade. RSVP stands for "rapid serial visual presentation." At the time of its development, programmers thought that it was possible to minimize saccades by flashing words at the reader at a constant rate. Sadly, nobody explained to those programmers how reading works in most reader's brains; how the meaning of the written text exists in paragraphs, and how punctuation helps with comprehension.

RSVP apps are plentiful and serve as fun demonstrations of a variety of reading speeds. We highly recommend checking them out. However, don't expect these apps to turn you into a speed reader.

One of our favorite speed reading apps slowly reveals the text to the reader, cluster by cluster, while the rest of the text is grayed out but still visible. This allows the reader to take advantage of peripheral vision and be able to divide ideas and concepts into paragraphs. This particular website is called *READFA.ST*, but it has many glitches, and we are unsure how long it will stick around on the web.

Useful Resources

For our Type 1 readers, we highly encourage you to practice reading every day. The 25-page-a-day suggestion applies to you the most. To make it easier on yourself, try to choose books on similar subjects so you can minimize new vocabulary and unfamiliar syntax roadblocks. When you pick up a new book, make sure it has a lot of overlap in style and content with the book you just finished reading. Obviously, we are not telling you to read the same books over and over again, but your brain must ease into the idea of speeding up and relaxing into a speed above 150 WPM with perfect comprehension.

You can always recheck your reading speed in your own material. After you calculate the average number of words per line, set the timer for one minute and read at your normal pace. Mark where you stopped and count the number of full lines you've read. For example, let's say that number is 10. Multiply the average word count per line (let's say 15) by the number of lines you read in a minute (10) to get your initial WPM (150 WPM). Once you graduate to the Type 2 reading level, you can open yourself up to a larger scope of books.

Our favorite websites for book suggestions are Goodreads and a personal blog by James Clear, where he makes great fiction and nonfiction book suggestions (jamesclear.com/best-books).

To explore the art of reading a book on a deeper level, check out a timeless masterpiece by Mortimer J. Adler titled *How to Read a Book.*

If you want to learn more about syntax and how meaning gets created, we suggest you check out *Artful Sentences: Syntax as Style,* by Virginia Tufte.

If you struggle with reading academic texts, we encourage you to check out a best-seller by Cathy Birkenstein and Gerald Graff called *They Say / I Say: The Moves That Matter in Academic Writing.*

Finally, you can find useful tips (including a demonstration of the palming technique) on my YouTube channel, *Seberson Method.*

References

Babauta, Leo. "A Guide to Habit Resilience." March 28, 2019. https://zenhabits.net/habit-resilience.

Babauta, Leo. "Chapter 2: The Age of Distraction." *Focus: A Simplicity Manifesto in the Age of Distraction*. Danville: Founders House, 2016.

Dreiser, Theodore. *The "Genius."* 1915.

Freeman, Marcia S., and Susan Koehler. *Models for Teaching Writing-craft Target Skills*. Gainesville, FL: Maupin House Pub., 2010.

Giovanni, Nikki, and Bryan Collier. *Rosa*. New York: Henry Holt, 2005.

Krieber, Magdalena, Katrin D. Bartl-Pokorny, Florian B. Pokorny, Christa Einspieler, Andrea Langmann, Christof Körner, Terje Falck-Ytter, and Peter B. Marschik. "The Relation between Reading Skills and Eye Movement Patterns in Adolescent Readers: Evidence from a Regular Orthography." National Center for Biotechnology Information, January 4, 2016. https://www.ncbi.nlm.nih.gov/pmc/articles/PMC4699816. Chapter 4: discussion regarding ". . . researchers noticed that their subjects fixated on groups of words at a time instead of individual words."

Rayner, Keith, Elizabeth R. Schotter, Michael E. J. Masson, Mary C. Potter, and Rebecca Treiman. "So Much to Read,

So Little Time: How Do We Read, and Can Speed Reading Help?" SAGE Journals, January 14, 2016. https://journals. sagepub.com/doi/full/10.1177/1529100615623267. Chapter 5: discussion regarding ". . . subvocalization is essential to reading comprehension."

Stevens, William K. "Speed Reading Has Become a Permanent Feature of Education in America." *New York Times*, September 19, 1971. https://www.nytimes. com/1971/09/19/archives/speed-reading-has-become -a-permanent-feature-of-education-in.html.

Tan, Li Hai, John Spinks, Guinevere Eden, Charles Perfetti, and Wai Ting Siok. "Reading depends on writing, in Chinese." National Center for Biotechnology Information, June 14, 2005. Chapter 1, Subvocalization Debate sidebar: discussion regarding "readers whose native language is non-alphabetic (Chinese or Tamil, for example) use their brains differently when reading."

Wolf, Maryanne. *Proust and the Squid: The Story and Science of the Reading Brain.* New York: HarperCollins Publishers, September 4, 2007.

Zacks Jeffrey M., and Rebecca Treiman. "Sorry, You Can't Speed Read." *New York Times*, April 15, 2016. https:// www.nytimes.com/2016/04/17/opinion/sunday /sorry-you-cant-speed read.html.

Index

Acknowledgments

First, I want to thank my editor, Justin Hartung, for being patient and remarkably accepting of my ideas. I want to give big thanks to Daniel and Beverly Bartfield for helping me navigate the process of becoming a writer. Thank you to all my students who provided me with ample opportunities for reading research and inquiry. Thank you to Andrey for understanding and adjusting to my crazy schedule while the book was being born. Thank you to my mom and grandmother for believing in me and rooting for me from another continent. Lastly, I want to give big thanks to Dr. Lois Bergman, who helped me understand the psychology of reading and decoding on a deeper level.

ABOUT THE AUTHOR

In search for better education and opportunity, Katya Seberson immigrated to the United States from Russia in 2007. After learning English in a fairly short period of time, she began the quest to reconcile her struggle with dyslexia and overcame her reading difficulties through self-experimentation and focused training. Katya has been involved with speed reading since college, where she worked as a speed reading instructor for one of the popular programs on the market. Through this experience, she gained valuable insights into the flaws of the industry and the level of training people were seeking. Over time, she developed her own methodology for effective reading and speed reading. The program quickly gained momentum, and client success stories spread like wildfire. Katya Seberson now owns a successful private practice in Manhattan, ExecutiveMind, where she teaches seminars and corporate workshops.